WHAT YOU NEED TO KNOW ABOUT

SALVATION

IN 12 LESSONS

MAX ANDERS

THOMAS NELSON PUBLISHERS
Nashville

Published in Nashville, Tennessee, by Thomas Nelson, Inc.

Unless otherwise indicated, Scripture quotations are from the *New King James Version of the Bible*, © 1979, 1980, 1982, 1990, Thomas Nelson, Inc., Publishers.

Scripture quotations identified by NASB are from the *New American Standard Bible*, © 1960, 1962, 1963, 1968, 1971, 1973, 1975, by the Lockman Foundation, and used by permission.

Scripture quotations identified by NIV are from the *Holy Bible, New International Version*, © 1973, 1978, 1984, by International Bible Society, and used by permission of Zondervan Bible Publishers.

Library of Congress Cataloging-in-Publication Data

Anders, Max E., 1947–
    Salvation: in twelve lessons/Max Anders.
        p.   cm. — (What you need to know about)
    Includes bibliographical references.
    ISBN 0-7852-1191-8
    1. Salvation—Biblical teaching.   I. Title.   II. Series: Anders,
    Max E., 1947-   What you need to know about.
BS680.S25A53   1998   97-48678
234—dc21   CIP

Printed in the United States of America

1 2 3 4 5 6 7 8—02 01 00 99 98

Contents

Introduction to the
What You Need to Know Series

You hold in your hands a tool with enormous potential—the ability to help ground you, and a whole new generation of other Christians, in the basics of the Christian faith.

I believe the times call for just this tool. We face a serious crisis in the church today . . . namely, a generation of Christians who know the truth but who do not live it. An even greater challenge is coming straight at us, however: a coming generation of Christians who may not even know the truth!

Many Christian leaders agree that today's evangelical church urgently needs a tool flexible enough to be used by a wide variety of churches to ground current and future generations of Christians in the basics of Scripture and historic Christianity.

This guide, and the whole series from which it comes—the *What You Need to Know* series—can be used by individuals or groups for just that reason.

Here are five other reasons why we believe you will enjoy using this guide:

1. It is easy to read.

You don't want to wade through complicated technical jargon to try to stumble on the important truths you are looking for. This series puts biblical truth right out in the open. It is written in a warm and friendly style, with even a smattering of humor here and there. See if you don't think it is different from anything you have ever read before.

2. It is easy to teach.

You don't have time to spend ten hours preparing for Sunday school, small group, or discipleship lessons. On the other hand, you don't want watered down material that insults your group's intellect. There is real meat in these pages, but it is presented in a way that is easy to teach. It follows a question-and-answer format that can be used to cover the material, along with discussion questions at the end of each chapter that make it easy to get group interaction going.

3. It is thoroughly biblical.

You believe the Bible, and don't want to use anything that isn't thoroughly biblical. This series has been written and reviewed by a team of people who are well-educated, personally committed Christians who have a high view of Scripture, and great care has been taken to reflect what the Bible teaches. If the Bible is unambiguous on a subject, such as the resurrection of Christ, then that subject is presented unambiguously.

4. It respectfully presents differing evangelical positions.

You don't want anyone forcing conclusions on you that you don't agree with. There are many subjects in the Bible on which there is more than one responsible position. When that is the case, this series presents those positions with respect, accuracy, and fairness. In fact, to make sure, a team of evaluators from various evangelical perspectives has reviewed each of the volumes in this series.

5. It lets you follow up with your own convictions and distinctives on a given issue.

You may have convictions on an issue that you want to communicate to the people to whom you are ministering. These books give you that flexibility. After presenting the various responsible positions that may be held on a given subject, you will find it easy then to identify and expand upon your view, or the view of your church.

We send this study guide to you with the prayer that God may use it to help strengthen His church for her work in these days.

How to Teach This Book

The books in this series are written so that they can be used as a thirteen-week curriculum, ideal for Sunday school classes or other small-group meetings. You will notice that there are only twelve chapters—to allow for a session when you may want to do something else. Every quarter seems to call for at least one different type of session, because of holidays, summer vacation, or other special events. If you use all twelve chapters, and still have a session left in the quarter, have a fellowship meeting with refreshments, and use the time to get to know others better. Or use the session to invite newcomers in hopes they will continue with the course.

All ten books in the series together form a "Basic Knowledge Curriculum" for Christians. Certainly Christians would eventually want to know more than is in these books, but they should not know less. Therefore, the series is excellent for seekers, for new Christians, and for Christians who may not have a solid foundation of biblical education. It is also a good series for those whose biblical education has been spotty.

Of course, the books can also be used in small groups and discipleship groups. If you are studying the book by yourself, you can simply read the chapters and go through the material at the end. If you are using the books to teach others, you might find the following guidelines helpful:

Teaching Outline

1. Begin the session with prayer.

2. Consider having a quiz at the beginning of each meeting over the self-test from the chapter to be studied for that day. The quiz can be optional, or the group may want everyone to commit to it, depending on the setting in which the material is

taught. In a small discipleship group or one-on-one, it might be required. In a larger Sunday school class, it might need to be optional.

3. At the beginning of the session, summarize the material. You may want to have class members be prepared to summarize the material. You might want to bring in information that was not covered in the book. There might be some in the class who have not read the material, and this will help catch them up with those who did. Even for those who did read it, a summary will refresh their minds and get everyone into a common mind-set. It may also generate questions and discussion.

4. Discuss the material at the end of the chapters as time permits. Use whatever you think best fits the group.

5. Have a special time for questions and answers, or encourage questions during the course of discussion. If you are asked a question you can't answer (it happens to all of us), just say you don't know, but that you will find out. Then, the following week, you can open the question and answer time, or perhaps the discussion time, with the answer to the question from last week.

6. Close with prayer.

You may have other things you would like to incorporate, and flexibility is the key to success. These suggestions are given only to guide, not to dictate. Prayerfully, choose a plan suited to your circumstances.

I remember two things: that I am a great sinner and that Christ is a great Savior.

■ John Newton (1725–1807), former slave trader and author of the hymn "Amazing Grace"

1

Are We Really Lost?

Imagine the scene in Tombstone, Arizona Territory, 1882. Jake Slade was in jail for stealing $10,000 worth of silver ore from the Silver Lady Mine. According to the law, Jake was guilty. But according to Jake, he was innocent. Oh, yes, he had taken the ore, but he did not consider it stealing. The man who owned the mine, Bill Mallory, had cheated Jake out of that much money and more in the past. Jake had worked for him, risked his life for him, and Bill was to have rewarded him with stock in the mine. He didn't. Now, in Jake's mind, he was only getting what belonged to him. But he got caught, and he was waiting in the jail for the territorial judge to come by next month to try the case.

In the meantime, Bill Mallory was not taking any chances. He did not want Jake's claim to stock in the silver mine to be brought up in court. There were those who had heard Bill promise Jake the silver stock. For a price, they were keeping their mouths shut for now, but Mallory didn't know what would happen if they were put under oath and threatened with perjury.

So Mallory concocted a scheme. He paid Slim Wilson, a casual friend of Jake's, to pay Jake a visit in jail and trick him into thinking that Slim would bust him out of the jail. Then he paid the sheriff to let it happen, but to be ready for Jake's escape.

"Listen," hissed Slim in Jake's ear. "I was just over to the Silver Slipper Saloon, and I heard that Bill Mallory has paid off the judge! He's going to throw the book at you. They're saying you'll go to prison for ten years for stealing that silver!"

"Why, that dirty, low-down snake in the grass!" Jake growled.

"You can say that again," sympathized Slim.

Jake stared at the floor as the news begin to sink in. Suddenly, he looked up at the messenger. "What am I going to do, Slim? I can't go to jail for ten years. I'd be an old man when I got out."

"Well, I don't know, Jake. Looks like you're in a heap a trouble. How 'bout if I get a couple of the boys to help me? I'll get your horse, and tonight after the sheriff goes to sleep, we'll tie some ropes around the bars in the window and pull the bars out. You jump out and get on your horse and ride west. Us boys can high-tail it east out of town and go on home. Our wives can say we were home all night. I think that would work."

"Okay," said Jake. "Let's do it. I'll see you tonight about midnight. And Slim—thanks. You're a real friend."

That night, Slim and the boys busted Jake out of jail. Everything went according to plan, Jake thought. Except that when he got on his horse and rounded the corner at full gallop heading west out of town, the sheriff stepped out of the shadows and shot him dead. At sunup the next morning, they put him six feet under on Boot Hill.

The very avenue that Jake thought would save him was the avenue that killed him. It was all a great deception, planned ahead of time and foisted on Jake. Essentially, Jake was dead the moment he believed the lie.

In this chapter we learn that . . .

1. The history of humanity's savagery against itself shows that humanity is lost.
2. Our conscience shows that we are lost since we are unable to live up to our own standards, let alone God's.
3. The inability of humanity to experience the fullness of its aspirations indicates its lostness.
4. Christ would not have endured the cross if humanity were not lost and in need of salvation.
5. The Bible says that all have sinned and come short of the glory of God and that the wages of that sin is eternal separation from God.

And so it is with humanity. Most people do not believe that they will die and go to hell. They think that something will save them. They think that either there is no hell, or there is no God, or that a loving God would not send them to hell, or that their good works will outweigh their bad. But those are all lies, deceptions of the devil. And in reality, we are doomed the moment we believe the lie. Like Jake, all we have to do is round the corner of life with our last heartbeat, and Satan steps out of the shadows and shoots us dead.

But since most people believe the lie that they are not in danger of going to hell, we have to start by asking the question, "Are we really lost?" The majority of people do not believe they are. But what we believe means absolutely nothing unless *God* believes the same thing. So, to try to gain God's perspective on the issue, we will ask several questions to see if the answers will give us insight on whether or not we are really lost and in need of salvation.

How Does History Show that We Are Lost?

The history of humanity's savagery against itself shows that humanity is lost.

We must begin by asking what we mean by "lost" and "saved." By "lost" we mean that our relationship with God is broken by our sin, and when we die, we will go to hell. By "saved," we mean that our relationship with God has been restored through faith in Jesus Christ and we will go to heaven.

Of course, that assumes that there is a God. If there is not a God, then we cannot be lost and we cannot be saved. We just live and die, and then we cease to exist. But if there is a God, then we might be lost and we might need to be saved. For the last two thousand years, one of the foundation stones of the Christian faith is that there is a God, humanity is lost, and everyone needs to be saved.

But is there any evidence outside the Bible to suggest that humanity is lost and in need of salvation? I think so. Just as you can tell something of what a tree is like by looking only at its shadow, perhaps we can tell something of what the spiritual side of humanity is like by looking at the physical side.

First, the entire story of history tells an endless succession of civilizations that rise on good principles, and then fall due to corruption. Rise and fall, rise and fall. There has never been a civilization that has risen and stayed there. Like daylilies in the July heat, civilizations bloom for a moment and then die. Why? Because of internal corruption. No great civilization ever fell because of external forces. They always fall from internal corruption.

Why I Need to Know This

I need to know this because otherwise I might erroneously conclude, as much of the world has, that I am not lost and have no need of salvation.

Humanity does not seem to be able to withstand prosperity. It breeds ingratitude and laziness and corruption. Within the very flower of cultural prosperity are the seeds of its own destruction.

Chief Seattle, for whom the city of Seattle, Washington, is named, lived from 1786 to 1866. He was friendly to the white settlers of his time. Yet he saw that in the coming of the white man, the seeds of destruction were sown for his own people. In a remarkably insightful statement toward the end of his life, he lamented the passing of his people and their civilization:

> A few more moons; a few more winters—and not one of the descendants of the mighty hosts that once moved over this broad land or lived in happy homes, protected by the Great Spirit, will remain to mourn over the graves of a people once more powerful and hopeful than yours (white men's). But why should I mourn at the untimely fate of my people? Tribe follows tribe, and nation follows nation, like the waves of the sea. It is the order of nature, and regret is useless. Your time of decay may be distant, but it will surely come, for even the White Man, whose God walked and talked with him as friend with friend, cannot be exempt from the common destiny. We may be brothers after all. We will see.

From ancient Egypt, to Israel, to Babylonia, to Persia, to Greece, to Rome, to Europe, to the United States, history is the tale of the rise of great civilizations, and their fall because of moral, social, and cultural degeneration. Does this suggest that humanity is basically good?

Then, there is also the rise of evil civilizations, always led by evil men. Nero, Genghis Khan, Adolf Hitler, Joseph Stalin, and Mao Tse-tung together are responsible for killing over 150 million people and torturing and ravaging hundreds of millions more (see *What If Jesus Had Never Been Born*, James Kennedy, chapter 15). Do these men suggest that humanity is basically good?

In our own country today, a nation founded with many Christian principles, the problems that we face today as a nation are beyond our ability to solve. Just fifty years ago, the major problems in schools were "talking out loud," "running in the halls," and "chewing gum." Today, the major problems are physical violence, sexual promiscuity, and drugs. Who has a solution that can take us back to the days when our problems were so minor? Who knows the path to return us to the time when we all agreed on a moral code that made metal detectors, undercover police, and a call for condom distribution in high schools unnecessary? Who can solve just this one problem in education?

No one.

Unless God brings renewal, unless God brings a great awakening, unless God stirs our hearts to return to Him and to the princples in His word, those days will never be seen in America again.

Society's problems are beyond our ability to solve.

Add to that the profound problems of drug and alcohol abuse, sexually transmitted diseases, physical and sexual abuse, divorce, gang violence, terrorism, corruption in business and politics, and the problems are compounded beyond comprehension. These are all problems that we cannot solve, because they are problems of the heart. Politics or armies cannot change the human heart.

What does that tell us? If there is a God, if there is a heaven, if there is a hell, what does that tell us? What does that shadow tell us about the tree? Is that the record of basic goodness? Is that the record of a people who are so good that they will automatically get into heaven?

We have had over four thousand years of recorded history, and it all suggests that while there is good in humanity, nevertheless, humanity is inherently and fatally flawed, and in need of salvation. History does not suggest that humanity is inherently good. History suggests the opposite.

How Does Our Conscience Show that We Are Lost?

Our conscience shows that we are lost since we are unable to live up to our own standards, let alone God's.

What does our own conscience tell us about our goodness? Do you sometimes do things even though you know they are wrong? Do you sometimes fail to do things, even though you know they are right? Are you a perfect human being, even by your own standards, let alone God's?

The Christian doctrine of the depravity of man (humanity) does not hold that humanity is incapable of doing good. Obviously, humanity is capable of doing great good. Look at the hospitals, look at the orphanages, look at the disaster relief that do good for humanity all around the world. Yes, humanity is capable of doing good. But at the same time, we are incapable of not doing evil. The same person who administrates an orphanage, doing good for hundreds of children, may go home and physically abuse his own child. The politician who is responsible for getting a hospital built for disadvantaged rural people may take a bribe from a construction company. Even the preacher who proclaims the gospel on Sunday morning may be hard and insensitive toward his wife.

Have you ever tried to be perfect? Have you ever tried to live up to your own standards, let alone God's standard of perfection? Have you ever said, "From this day on, I will do all the good I am able, and I will refrain from doing wrong." If you have, you know that you are incapable of doing it. If you haven't tried it, try it. It will not be long before you go down in defeat.

I came to the conclusion, early in my Christian experience, as I tried to be perfect, that I could make myself do almost anything I wanted to *except* desire to do only good all the time. My "wanter" is basically flawed. And even if it weren't, I still don't believe I could perform perfectly. It just isn't in me. It isn't in anyone.

None of us is perfect. Do you think heaven is a perfect place? If you do, and if you are not perfect, how will you get there? How can the imperfect be joined to the perfect? Either the imperfect cannot be joined to the perfect, or else the perfect becomes corrupted by being joined with the imperfect. Neither one can be true if heaven is to be a perfect place where we can live with God forever.

So what is the solution? There is only one. We must become perfect. We must admit that we are lost and in need of the salvation God offers, and ask Him to forgive our sins and makes us spiritually perfect.

How Does Our Experience Show that We Are Lost?

The inability of humanity to experience the fullness of its aspirations indicates its lostness.

Most people are working on a game plan for meaning and purpose in life. It may be on a vast scale or on a simple and personal level, but most of us are looking to this world to give us a sense of purpose and meaning. We may be working up the career ladder or amassing a formidable education we believe will deliver professional success, or a love relationship we hope will make life complete or a new home or third car or sailboat or other "toy" that we think will make us happy and fulfilled. But many people discover that if they get what they want from this world, it doesn't satisfy. An emptiness seeps up from somewhere deep within, and a muffled alarm sounds that will not go away. The phrase, "Is this really all there is?" chimes on the hour and grows into a relentless reminder of the futility of life. Lee Iaccoca, the wildly successful former head of both Ford and Chrysler Motors, said, "Fame and fortune is for the birds."

But there are others who don't succeed in life. They don't come close to their aspirations. They compare their life twenty years after graduation and see that life has not at all turned out the way they thought or hoped it would. A pervasive and inescapable sense of futility, of powerlessness, of victimization assaults them, convincing them that the world is truly a fallen place, and humanity truly a fallen race, both in need of deliverance and unable to deliver themselves.

Oscar Wilde once said, "In this world there are only two tragedies. One is not getting what one wants, and the other is getting it." Either way, people discover somehow that things aren't right. They might not describe themselves as "lost," but they would agree that they need an answer from outside themselves, a power greater than themselves. If someone is looking for such an answer, he is lost and in need of the answer salvation through Christ brings.

How Does the Death of Christ Show that We Are Lost?

Christ would not have endured the cross if humanity were not lost and in need of salvation.

History, conscience, and personal experience show that humanity has critical needs that it is unable to meet, dilemmas from which it needs to be saved. Christians believe that the salvation that perfectly fits humanity's deepest needs and most difficult dilemmas is given through Jesus Christ and especially through His unique, powerful death.

The death that Jesus died on the cross was a truly horrible death. First, there was the physical agony. Can you imagine having been beaten until His face was so swollen and disfigured that He was not readily recognizable? They pulled out His beard and spit on Him. They jammed a crown of thorns into His skull, which would have been like having a bunch of small, sharp nails driven through your skin and lodged into the bone in your skull. They whipped Him until His back bled. Then, they made Him carry His own cross until He was so exhausted He could not carry it anymore.

When He arrived at the place of crucifixion, they drove nails through His hands and feet. But this is worse than we think at first. These nails were not the smooth construction nails that we know today. They were more like small railroad spikes, squared off instead of round, and ragged on the edges. And they nailed them, not through His hands and feet, which would have been bad enough, but through His wrist and ankles, ripping and tearing the flesh and cartillage, and dislodging the small bones in those areas.

The only way He could breathe was to push up on His feet, which had the nails driven through them. It was one agony if He did, and another agony if He didn't. He hung there for hours, until, mercifully, He died.

And this He did voluntarily. It would have been gruesome under any circumstances. But He did not have to go through the crucifixion. He could have saved Himself. Others who were crucified endured it because they had to. He endured it because He wanted to, for our sake. What would have motivated Him to go through that?

Jesus' agony on the cross was both physical and spiritual.

Second, there is the spiritual agony. That which is holy (Jesus) must be horrified with that which is unholy (sin). Yet, on the cross, Jesus had the sin of the world placed on Him. What must that have been like? What kind of agony might that have created?

It must have offended and horrified Him, just as we are offended and horrified by things that violate our sensibility. Let me try to walk on a very razor edge of reality to get a glimpse of what Jesus suffered, I hope, without offending you.

As an example, I will never forget hearing the account of a young woman in New York who was assaulted by a man in a dark residential street. She screamed for help. It was a hot summer night, and hundreds of people, whose windows were open, heard her. The man raped her. Then he stabbed her repeatedly with a knife. All the time the woman was screaming, crying, and begging for someone to help her. She continued to scream as he continued to stab the knife into her body again and again, dozens of times. Finally the screams died out. Her life blood oozed out on the sidewalk as the killer fled into the night. No one even called the police. They didn't want to get involved.

I was horrified. I was repulsed. I was offended.

Let me give you another example. I will never forget traveling home from my first year in seminary with a friend. We were talking and laughing and reminiscing when a car, driving erratically, pulled up beside us. Then it veered strangely over into the median of the interstate, where it smashed through a guard rail and plunged twenty feet down into a rocky river bed. As other cars stopped, my friend and I sped to the nearest house to call an ambulance and the police. Then, because we were witnesses, and thought that we might be needed to give a report to the police, we returned to the accident site just in time to watch an emergency worker carry the white, lifeless form of a four-year-old child up onto the grass and cover it with a blanket.

I was horrified. I was repulsed. I was offended.

I remember as a youth during the Vietnam war watching on television the atrocities of war being brought right into my living room. I remember watching on live television a Vietnamese deserter being brought up to a platform before hundreds of witnesses. They made him face the crowd. Then, a man walked up to him, put a gun to his head and pulled the trigger. The deserter dropped in a heap at his feet.

I was horrified. I was repulsed. I was offended.

Our horror at sin only suggests what Jesus experienced.

I believe Jesus was infinitely more horrified, repulsed, and offended when the sin of the world was placed on Him at the cross. I do not mean to suggest that Jesus' experience on the cross is exactly the same as our experience of outrage and horror upon hearing a disturbing story. It is surely much greater than that. I am just trying to find a way of portraying the fact that we don't have to do something, or even experience something to feel assaulted, violated, crushed, and stricken by it. All we have to do is *hear* about it. If that is true with us, then it is true of Jesus. He did not have to commit sin, but simply come in contact with it in the mystical way He did on the cross, in order for it to have created profound anguish and suffering of soul and spirit. He is totally holy, and we are not. He had all the sin of the whole world placed on Him, whereas we have only limited sin. The agony must have been unspeakable. He saw all the pain, all the evil, all the suffering of all people who have ever lived in the past, who were alive at the time, and who will ever live. It was placed on Him in some mysterious way we do not fully understand. But we understand our horror at these three examples that I gave, and we cannot even imagine the horror He suffered as a Holy God was touched by sin and death.

Why would Jesus have endured that? After all, He didn't have to. In John 10:18, we read, "No one takes [my life] from Me, but I lay it down." He could have called ten thousand angels to destroy the world and set Him free. Why would He have en-

Jesus did not have to endure the cross.

dured the unimaginable physical agony, and why would He have endured the unimaginable spiritual horror if it were not for some colossal reason? Would He have endured it if humanity were basically good and not in need of salvation? Would He have done it if humanity could have had its sin overlooked and would have gone to heaven anyway, without His suffering and death? It is unthinkable. The crucifixion is only explainable to me if humanity is lost. It only makes sense to me if, being motivated by a profound love for us, Jesus decided to die in our place, so we could live in His. For me, no other explanation is adequate.

What Does the Bible Say about Humanity's Lostness?

The Bible says that all have sinned and come short of the glory of God and that the wages of that sin is eternal separation from God.

Having looked at other evidence to suggest humanity's lostness, we now turn to the statements of Scripture. If we take the Bible at face value, we simply cannot avoid the fact that humanity is lost and in need of personal salvation. In Romans, two verses combine with particular force: "For all have sinned and fall short of the glory of God" (Romans 3:23) and "For the wages of sin is death, but the gift of God is eternal life in Christ Jesus our Lord" (Romans 6:23).

But the Bible by no means stops there:

> For God so loved the world that He gave His only begotten Son, that whoever believes in Him should not perish but have everlasting life. For God did not send His Son into the world to condemn the world, but that the world through Him might be saved. He who believes in Him is not condemned; but he who does not believe is condemned already, because he has not believed in the name of the only begotten Son of God. (John 3:16–18)

As Jesus was contrasting the actions of the redeemed with the unredeemed in Matthew 25:41, He was unambiguous in His description of the fate of those who reject Him: "Then He will also say to those on His left hand, 'Depart from Me, you cursed, into the everlasting fire prepared for the devil and his angels.' "

In Acts 4:12 we read, "Nor is there salvation in any other; for there is no other name under heaven given among men by which we must be saved."

In Romans 5:8–10, we read: "But God demonstrates His own love toward us, in that while we were still sinners, Christ died for us. Much more then, having now been justified by His blood, we shall be saved from wrath through Him. For if when we were enemies we were reconciled to God through the death of His Son, much more, having been reconciled, we shall be saved by His life."

And finally, we read in Ephesians 2:1–10:

> And you He made alive, who were dead in trespasses and sins, in which you once walked according to the course of this world, according to the prince of the power of the air, the spirit who now works in the sons of disobedience, among whom also we all once conducted ourselves in the lusts of our flesh, fulfilling the desires of the flesh and of the mind, and were by nature children of wrath, just as the others. But God, who is rich in mercy, because of His great love with which He loved us, even when we were dead in trespasses, made us alive together with Christ (by grace you have been saved), and raised us up together, and made us sit together in the heavenly places in Christ Jesus, that in the ages to come He might show the exceeding riches of His grace in His kindness toward us in Christ Jesus. For by grace you have been saved through faith, and that not of yourselves; it is the gift of God, not of works, lest anyone should boast.

Conclusion

Romans 5:10 says, "For if when we were enemies we were reconciled to God through the death of His Son, much more, having been reconciled, we shall be saved by His life." From this we learn that to be lost is to be in a state unreconciled to God, and to be saved means to be reconciled to God by believing in Jesus and receiving the forgiveness of our sins which He offers us by grace through faith.

We see, then, lessons from history and the testimony of our own conscience show that humanity is unreconciled to God. We are not sinners because we sin. Rather, we sin because we are sinners. David said in Psalm 51:5, "Behold, I was brought forth in iniquity,/ And in sin my mother conceived me." This does not mean that his mother committed sin in the act of conceiving David. Rather, it means that from the moment of conception, the flaw, the corruption of sin was in him. We are all born with it. And if we die with it, we are eternally lost. But if we repent and commit our lives to Christ, our sins are forgiven and we are saved—we live with God and His children in peace, love, and joy in heaven forever.

We are really lost. But we really can be saved.

Speed Bump

Slow down to be sure you've gotten the main points of this chapter.

Question
Answer

Q1. How does history show that we are lost?

A1. The history of humanity's *savagery* against itself shows that humanity is lost.

Q2. How does our conscience show that we are lost?

A2. Our conscience shows that we are lost since we are *unable* to live up to our own standards, let alone God's.

Q3. How does our experience show that we are lost?

A3. The inability of humanity to experience the *fullness* of its aspirations indicates its lostness.

Q4. How does the death of Christ show that we are lost?

A4. Christ would not have *endured* the cross if humanity were not lost and in need of salvation.

Q5. What does the Bible say about humanity's lostness?

A5. The Bible says that all have sinned and come short of the glory of God and that the wages of that sin is eternal *separation* from God.

Fill in the Blank

Question
Answer

Q1. How does history show that we are lost?

A1. The history of humanity's _____ against itself shows that humanity is lost.

Q2. How does our conscience show that we are lost?

A2. Our conscience shows that we are lost since we are _____ to live up to our own standards, let alone God's.

Q3. How does our experience show that we are lost?

A3. The inability of humanity to experience the _____ of its aspirations indicates its lostness.

Q4. How does the death of Christ show that we are lost?

A4. Christ would not have _____ the cross if humanity were not lost and in need of salvation.

Q5. What does the Bible say about humanity's lostness?

A5. The Bible says that all have sinned and come short of the glory of God and that the wages of that sin is eternal _____ from God.

For Further Thought and Discussion

1. What acts or characteristics of humanity have you witnessed that suggest to you that humanity is lost and in need of salvation?

2. What percentage of the time do you think you live a perfect life? What does that suggest about your standing before a perfect and holy God?

3. Would you go through what Jesus did if it were not necessary? Would you endure what He endured just to provide a good example of a life lived for others? Can you think of any explanation that would account for Jesus' willingness to be crucified other than His compassion and love for us as being lost and without hope?

4. What impact does the rather clear statement from Scriptures have on you that all have sinned and come short of the glory of God, and that the penalty of that sin is eternal separation from God?

What If I Don't Believe?

If I don't believe, I may ignore the warnings of the Bible, the testimony of history, and the conclusion of my own conscience, and go through life without ever receiving Jesus as my personal Savior. I might believe the lie of the devil and round the corner of life only to have him step out of the shadows and shoot me dead. If I believe God and trust Him, and obey Him, and I am wrong, I have lost nothing. But if I don't believe Him, trust Him, and obey Him, and I am wrong, I will have lost everything.

For Further Study

1. Scripture

- Matthew 25:41
- John 3:16–18
- Acts 4:12
- Romans 5:8–10
- Ephesians 2:1–12

2. Books

How to Be Born Again, Billy Graham
Know What You Believe, Paul Little

When God scooped up a handful of dust,
And spit on it, and molded the shape of man,
And blew a breath into it and told it to walk—
That was a great day.
■ Carl Sandburg (1878–1967)

What Did God Have in Mind when He Created?

A friend of mine once vividly described to me a wedding he had attended. It was a glorious affair. The sanctuary was a beautiful cathedral with granite walls, dazzling stained-glass windows, solid mahogany pews and pulpit, and a brass cross on the altar that was probably twenty feet high.

The wedding party was very large. There were a dozen bridesmaids in exquisite flowing gowns, a dozen groomsmen in tails and white ties, a flower girl, and a ring bearer. The sanctuary was filled with well-dressed and adoring friends and relatives.

In addition to the traditional organ, there was also a small brass and string ensemble playing classical music. One would have thought that a minor figure of royalty was getting married.

As the music played for the dozen bridesmaids to walk down the seemingly unending aisle of the large sanctuary, it started out very soft and gradually began building in depth, breadth, and volume, until by the time the last bridesmaid was at the altar, the music was loud and full. Then, three trumpeters stood and pealed out an ear-splitting fanfare worthy of a reigning monarch, at the end of which the organ began for the bride a deafening prelude that started the teeth of the guests in the front rows buzzing, while those sitting in the back rows began vibrating down to one end of the pews. At the grand moment, the audience stood in anticipation of the appearance of the bride. The organ was all-stops out and full volume, as the organist hammered the black and white keys mercilessly. The string ensemble sawed furiously at their instruments as the brass ensemble, neck veins bulging and eyes popping, tried to raise the dead.

My friend was so taken aback by the extraordinary fanfare of it all that it seemed the only thing the bride could possibly have done to

equal the dramatic crescendo would have been to swing down out of
the balcony on a rope, releasing her grip at the critical moment so
that, after doing a double back flip, she landed precisely beside the
waiting groom! As it was, her customary entrance was an anticlimax.
Had she been able to generate a halo, or walk slightly above the
ground, it would have been different—she might have been able to
do justice to the build-up. But it was not to be. Her entrance was un-
derwhelming.

In this chapter we learn that . . .

1. God created to reveal His glory.
2. God intended to populate the world with people with whom He could
   share His love and reveal His glory forever.
3. God intended the world to reflect His character and His glory.

It was a glorious affair, but the glory exceeded the reality. There is
a level of glory that is appropriate for humanity, and after it is exceeded, we call it "hype." We see it every year at Super Bowl time.
The Super Bowl is, perhaps, the ultimate hype in America. It is only a
football game. It is usually a blowout—not even interesting. Yet it has
achieved the status of a national holiday, largely because of the media
hype surrounding it.

So, when we read in the Bible that God created the universe for
His glory, we wonder what that means. Is it hype? Is it mere
pageantry to show off someone who is really no better than we are?
Why does God want to get glory for Himself? Is He a great cosmic
egomaniac who wants a race of servants who will grovel forever at
His feet? Is that why God wants glory? Is there more to the glory of
God than there is to the glory of men?

There is.

In answer to these and other questions, we need to explore what
God had in mind when He created. To do so, we will ask and answer
three key questions.

Why Did God Create in the First Place?
God created to reveal His glory.

Throughout the Scripture, we see the idea that God created
the universe and all that is in it to reveal His glory. But someone

might ask, "Why did He want to reveal His glory?" To that question we may not have an answer. When we begin to plumb the depths of God, we run out of plumb line long before we get to the bottom. Everything eventually dissolves into silence or mystery. However, just because we cannot know everything about God does not mean we cannot know anything.

The Bible says that humanity is created in the image of God, and if we can learn anything about God by looking at humanity, the pinnacle of His creation, we might speculate that "creating" is one of the innate characteristics of God. Just as God is good and loving and just, so He also may be "creative." Therefore He creates because it is part of His perfect nature to create. If that is so, then He created the universe as an expression of His essential nature.

To give an analogy, I know a number of creative people. Some are artists, some are musicians, some are singers, some are putterers in their woodworking shops, but they all have one thing in common. They seem incapable of *not* creating. It is just *in* them, and it comes out as a natural course of living their lives.

I even find a minor capacity for "creating" in myself. I do things just because I love to do them. Sometimes I sing, just for the pure fun of singing. I hum to myself, or sing under my breath as I go about other duties. Sometimes I take inordinate pleasure in whistling. In comparison with others, I am a better whistler than I am singer. I am embarrassed to sing in front of others, but I am not embarrassed to whistle in front of them. If I eat potato chips or something salty, it makes my lips very soft and pliable and I can whistle like crazy. Sometimes when I whistle by myself, I get so caught up in the process of making the sound and enjoying the melody that I become a human canary, whistling my head off for the pure pleasure of it.

Also, I have a strong urge to paint. I particularly enjoy watercolors. I took a class one time at a local university in watercoloring and was surprised at how bad I was. Everything I painted looked like a storm at sea. I despaired of ever doing it right. However, even that disappointing experience did not completely banish my yearning to create, and a number of years later, I visited the home of a very talented watercolor artist. She worked magic with a paint brush. I asked her if she ever gave lessons. She said she did. So my wife and I began taking lessons from her. And, to my surprise, she was able to get me to paint something that did not look like a storm at sea. I will never be famous or rich from painting, but I just enjoy doing it. I enjoy creating beauty, and reflecting my interests, likes and desires.

If that natural bent to create is part of humanity, perhaps it was put there by God because it is part of God's nature and we are created in His image.

Another reason why God created may be found in His characteristic of love. Scripture makes it clear that God is love (1 John 4:8). Several other passages make it clear that one of the central characteristics of love is that it "gives." In John 3:16, we read that

Creativity seems to be part of God's nature.

"God so loved the world that He *gave* His only begotten Son." In Ephesians 5:25, we read, "Husbands, love your wives just as Christ also loved the church and gave Himself for it."

From these passages that state it clearly, and many other passages that exemplify it, we see that "love" "gives". If it is love, it gives. It if doesn't give, it is not love. This is a powerful observation for the realm of human love, but an even more powerful observation concerning God's act of creation. One of the reasons God created may be so that He could love and give to us forever (Ephesians 2:7).

This is hard for us to grasp because we find it easier to be ungrateful for the temporal things God has not given us than to be grateful for the eternal things He *has* given us. After the initial impact has worn off, it is hard for us to receive emotional funding from the fact that our sins are forgiven, that we are accepted in Christ, that we have a home in heaven, that we will be separated from our sin eternally, that we can fellowship with God and each other forever unhindered by sin. We know these things are true, but we take greater immediate pleasure if we get a good job, make a lot of money, marry a pleasing spouse and rear children who delight us, and live happy, healthy, unfrustrated lives.

We are like a child who is unhappy that his parents will not buy him a new bicycle, unable to appreciate the fact that they are saving money for his college education. The bicycle is not nearly as important as the college education, but to the immature child, the education is not nearly so rewarding at the moment.

In the act of human procreation, we may see this bent to love and give. If you ask a loving mother why she wanted to have a baby, she might be hard-pressed to put it into words, but the desire is just "in there." We want to extend ourselves. We want to

---

Why I Need to Know This

I need to know this so that I will begin to appreciate what God has done. The original creation was glorious beyond our ability to imagine. His re-creation, both through the Christians' new birth as well as in the new heavens and the new earth, will very likely surpass the original. We need to be glad for what He has done. And, we need to be certain we do not look at the evil, the pain, the disappointment of this present fallen world and think any less of God or disparage creation. The sin and evil that have taken creation hostage are not God's doing. His response to these is salvation, the Great Rescue, which will cause creation to fulfill God's original purposes for it. In the end, all will be well.

---

create life and give goodness to that life. Every responsible parent wants to do what is right for his child, to help his child become all that he/she can be, and reflect the good values of the parent.

And where do we find greater joy than when someone tells us that he likes our picture, or likes the song we sang (or whistled), or that our child is a remarkable child? What joy we take when someone else values that which we create!

While this is not a complete answer, it may put us on the right track for a fuller understanding of why God created. Perhaps He created because it is part of His nature to create. He did not need to create, but of His own free will He chose to create, and because He is God His creation is going to be the best. If God is going to do His best, He is going to reflect Himself in His creation, and is going to bring glory to Himself.

In Isaiah 43:7, we read that God created His "sons and daughters" *for my glory.* In 1 Corinthians 10:31 we read, "Whether you eat or drink or whatever you do, do all to the glory of God." So, our lives are to be dedicated to His glory. The church is to give God glory (Ephesians 3:21); one day every knee shall bow and every tongue confess that Jesus Christ is Lord, to the glory of God (Philippians 2:11); in all things, God is to be glorified (1 Peter 4:11); and in heaven, the glory of God will be a central theme as we see in Revelation 5:13: "Blessing and honor and *glory* and power be to Him who sits on the throne."

So, yes, God wants us to give Him glory. But is He a celestial egomaniac who wants a race of serfs who will grovel at His feet for eternity to satisfy a raging ego? Hardly. In fact, the Bible makes it clear that God wants to give glory to humanity. You may be tempted to skip over these passages, but I encourage you to read them.

> For I consider that the sufferings of this present time are not worthy to be compared with the glory which shall be revealed in us. (Romans 8:18)
>
> But we speak the wisdom of God in a mystery, the hidden wisdom which God ordained before the ages for our glory. (1 Corinthians 2:7)
>
> For our light affliction, which is but for a moment, is working for us a far more exceeding and eternal weight of glory. (2 Corinthians 4:17)
>
> When Christ who is our life appears, then you also will appear with Him in glory. (Colossians 3:4)

These and other passages teach us that God intends to share His glory with us. *As we give glory to God, God gives glory to us. When we withhold glory from God, God withholds glory from us.*

God not only created humanity to give glory to Him, but He also created the physical universe for His glory. In Psalm 19:1, we read, "The heavens declare the glory of God." In Revelation 4:11, we read a song of heavenly worship that connects God's creation of all things with the fact that He is worthy to receive glory from them:

> You are worthy, O Lord,
> To receive glory and honor and power;
> For You created all things,
> And by Your will they exist and were created.

Serious thought about the magnificence of the human mind and body, one glance at the sun, moon, and stars, or brief inspection of a leaf on a tree convinces us of God's great wisdom, power, and right to receive glory, since He is the one responsible for it all. Who could make all this? Who could speak it into existence out of nothing? Who could exert the power necessary to keep it all going for countless centuries? The power, skill, knowledge, and wisdom are all beyond our mortal comprehension. When we think deeply about it, we give glory to God. There is no other response that is adequate.

Why Did God Create Humanity as He Did?

God intended to populate the world with people with whom He could share His love and reveal His glory forever.

Friends are at the very heart of what makes life worth living. Good friends can enrich us, encourage us, help us, counsel us, and just be *with* us. If my life were a continent, and I were flying over it, the highest mountains on that continent would be the good friends I've had—and have—over the years. I want to tell you about a few of them, though the names and circumstances will be changed to protect privacy.

First, I think of my family. They were my first friends. I had three sisters and two brothers, a mother and father. Until I went to school, my life revolved almost totally around them. As part of something larger than myself, I belonged. My fondest memories were of our family—all eight of us—sitting around the supper table, talking, laughing, sharing our stories of the day. I remember my dad making us laugh. He was funny! And so were several of my brothers and sisters. Like any family, we had our quarrels and disagreements, but underneath it all, we were friends.

Then, when I went to school, Allen and I became great friends. One of our great joys was when we went camping and fishing together. We had a flawless routine. We would get to the campsite at the lake Friday after school, and by the time we got the tent pitched, campfire built, and all the gear stowed, it was too late to fish. So, even though we planned to eat nothing but fish, we would break out the hot dogs and beans and marshmallows, sit around the fire, eating enough to supply a small army, and talk late into the night. We would go to bed very late, planning to get up before daybreak in the morning to catch the fish. But we always overslept. So, we'd get up around 10:00 and, since there were no fish to eat, would scramble eggs, fry bacon, make pancakes, and eat for an hour or so. Then, by the time we got everything cleaned up, it was too late to fish. So we'd go for a swim, then row around the lake, go exploring in the woods, shoot tin cans with our BB guns, and generally fritter the afternoon away. Then we'd start fishing as the sun was going down, but the mosquitoes were always so bad, they'd drive us back to the tent where we'd build a hot fire, then put leaves on it to create smoke which would drive away the mosquitoes.

Of course, by then, we were hungry again, so we'd roast some more hot dogs and, with beans and marshmallows, eat ourselves into oblivion. Then we'd talk late into the night about basketball, fishing, guns, and girls. Of course, we'd go to bed planning to get up very early in the morning to catch some fish. But the next day would go about like the first one.

On all our camping trips, we never ate a fish. But we did have fun!

Friends make life worth living. As I grew older and taller, my attention turned to basketball, and Joe became a good friend. We would play ball by the hour at his home or at the town park. We played on a Cinderella team in high school that was one of the better teams in the state. Then we went to different colleges, both on basketball scholarships. I went to a Christian college, and he went to a pagan college nearby, near enough that we played each other. The pagans always whipped us, and Joe helped them! It was demoralizing. It was like a Christian had joined the lions. But our friendship has lasted through the years.

Then there was Stuart in college, and Paul in seminary, and Dick and Al and Bill in my first ministries. Curt and Brian and another Brian were important to me in my first church, and Dave and Steve and Mike in my second church, and on it goes. New friends were added to the old, but none was lost.

Then there was the time several years ago when I became seriously ill. I was bedridden in a specialized clinic out of state. As the old joke goes, for a while, I was so sick I was afraid I would die, and then things got worse, and I was afraid I wouldn't. As I lay there, day after day, for months, I felt so isolated and vulnerable that I began to despair. My wife was at my bedside daily, trying to figure out what to do to help me. Unbeknownst to me, she had talked with another cherished friend who flew halfway across the United States to see me in one of my darkest moments. I was overwhelmed. It seemed almost as though God Himself had visited me in the skin of my friend. In ways that I don't fully understand, that was the turning point of my illness. Within another month, I left the clinic.

Finally, space is inadequate for me to get specific about my best friend, Margie. She is my wife, my friend, my comrade in arms, my spiritual intimate. What would life be without her?

Friends. Who can overstate their value, their worth? They

double our joy and divide our grief. Emerson once said, "We take care of our health, we lay up money, we make our roof tight and our clothing sufficient, but who provides wisely that he shall not be wanting in the best property of all—friends?" William James said, "Wherever you are, it is your friends who make your world." Charles Haddon Spurgeon wrote, "Friendship is one of the sweetest joys of life." Goethe wrote, "The world is so empty if one thinks only of mountains, rivers, and cities, but to know someone here and there who thinks and feels with us and who, though distant, is close to us in spirit, makes the whole earth a garden."

We say all this about friends as a backdrop to answer the question, "What did God have in mind when He created humanity?" The answer is, when all is said, He wanted a family of friends with whom He could share His love and His glory forever. In Romans 8:15–16, we read, "You received the Spirit of adoption by whom we cry out, 'Abba, Father.' The Spirit Himself bears witness with our spirit that we are children of God, and if children, then heirs—heirs of God and joint heirs with Christ, if indeed we suffer with Him, that we may also be glorified together."

> **Friendships provide a clue as to why God created humanity.**

In this passage, we see that we are children of God. As such, we may call him "Abba," which is a familiar term of endearment. It is close to "Daddy" or "Papa."

Continuing this relationship, we see, in John 15:15, Jesus' words, "No longer do I call you servants, for a servant does not know what his master is doing; but I have called you friends."

In this passage, Jesus, the second member of the Trinity, announces in no uncertain terms His willingness—no, desire—to have a relationship of friendship with His created beings.

Regarding this remarkable fact, James Packer has written, in his fine volume, *God Has Spoken:*

> God's purpose in revelation is to *make friends* with us. It was to this end that He created us rational beings, bearing His image, able to think and hear and speak and love; He wanted there to be genuine personal affection and friendship, two-sided, between Himself and us—a relation, not like that between a man and his dog, but like that of a father to his son, or a husband to his wife. Loving friendship between two persons has no ulterior motive; it is an end in itself. And this is God's end in revelation. He speaks to us simply to fulfill the

purpose for which we were made; that is, to bring into being a relationship in which He is a friend to us, and we to Him, He finding His joy in giving us gifts and we finding ours in giving Him thanks (50).

This concept dovetails into the point John Piper makes in *Desiring God*, when he clarifies the chief purpose of human existence. Slightly revising the famous answer to the first question in the Westminster Shorter Catechism, Piper says that the chief end of man is that he is to glorify God *by* enjoying Him forever. If we do not enjoy God, Piper says, we will not glorify Him; and we glorify Him fully only as we enjoy Him.

This apparently was what God had in mind when He created Adam and Eve. They walked with God and talked with Him directly. They lived in paradise, in fellowship and harmony with God. His intention was a glorious friendship, mutual love and common purpose that God had toward humanity in the beginning, and it is to restore that intention that He has been working ever since the fall.

Why Did God Create the World as He Did?

God intended the world to reflect His character and His glory.

In his book *How Should We Then Live?* theologian Francis Schaeffer placed successive self-portraits of Vincent Van Gogh. By looking at the portraits in chronological order, you could see Van Gogh go insane. His first portrait was fairly lifelike. Each successive one thereafter degenerated until the final one looked like a madman, because it was painted by a madman.

The point?

We can tell a lot about someone by what he creates. Tragically, when children today are asked to draw pictures, they often draw pictures of shootings or stabbings or skulls or aliens or demonic-looking creatures. There is often violence and blood in the pictures. How sad to see a culture degenerating before our very eyes in the pictures of our children.

What can we tell about God by looking at His creation? We discover two primary things—power and beauty.

As to God's power, who has not gazed at the starry heavens on a clear night and been overwhelmed by the awesomeness of space? There are a hundred billion stars in our galaxy, and perhaps a hundred billion galaxies that can be seen with our current telescopes. They all revolve with amazing precision. The size, the precision, the beauty all tell us about God.

God's creation reveals His power and beauty.

The heavens are so enormous that it is sometimes difficult to grasp what is "up there." As a child, I used to think the sky at night was a black bowl upside down with little pin holes poked in it to let light through from an unknown source behind the black bowl. Compared to what the heavens really are, my ability to grasp it all probably has not progressed significantly beyond that stage.

For another glimpse of God's power and beauty, consider the Grand Canyon. I had seen pictures of the Grand Canyon all the years I was growing up and was never particularly bedazzled by it. Then my wife and I moved to Arizona. I will never forget driving up to the canyon for the first time. The terrain does not prepare you for it. You drive through rather flat, pine-covered country for a little while. Then, you round a corner, crest a hill, and suddenly, THERE IT IS—the biggest hole in the ground on earth! I was dumbstruck. My mind could not take in what I was seeing. The first thing that went through my mind was, *Grand* Canyon? *Grand? Grand just doesn't do it.* We use the word "grand" for grand ballrooms of hotels, and grand opera or grand piano. If we use grand for all those rather diminutive objects, we need another whole word for the canyon I was looking at. Stupendous Canyon? Colossal Canyon? Knock-your-socks-off, can't-believe-your-eyes Canyon? It was beyond anything I could ever have prepared myself for. People have been known to burst into tears upon their first view of it. The Indian who was said to have discovered the canyon reportedly tied himself to a tree to keep from going mad at the sight.

If you have seen it, you know what I mean. If you have not seen it, let your mind run wild, and you will not envision half the reality.

The power of God is seen in the canyon. Yet, it is only a little blemish on the face of one of the planets in one of the solar systems of the galaxy. And God spoke it all into existence "from nothing." God is a great and powerful God—awesome in the true sense of the word. If it is God who created all this, and if we can know something of the artist by what he creates, then the universe tells us much about the greatness and power of God.

But let's go to the other extreme. In the remotest corners of the globe, some sites that are virtually never seen by the human eye are some of the most beautiful on earth. Why? Why would God "waste" such beauty where it will never be seen? Because God is a God of beauty, and when He creates, He creates beauty.

Charles Kuralt wrote, in his book *A Life on the Road*, about a time he stumbled upon thousands of acres of wildflowers. He had been interviewing people in Douglas, Wyoming, about jack-alopes, a curious combination of jackrabbit and antelope. It looks like a jackrabbit, except that it has the horns of an antelope. Non-natives believe it is a mythical creature, but natives swear (with tongue in cheek) that they are real. Douglas is the jacka-lope capital of the world.

Some of God's most awesome creations are rarely seen.

Kuralt's team decided to go on to Cheyenne to see what was going on there over the Fourth of July. They remembered Interstate 25 being a rather boring stretch of road between Douglas and Cheyenne, so they took off on a dirt road that goes about eighty miles over the hills of Medicine Bow. They had planned to take old U.S. 30 at Medicine Bow and still make it to Cheyenne in plenty of time for supper.

But they never made it to Cheyenne at all. A few miles out of Douglas, they started noticing wildflowers. It started out slowly at first. There were patches of daisies and wild geraniums, stands of mountain columbine at the bottoms of the hills that opened up to vast fields of Indian paintbrush on the slopes of the hills. The farther they went, the more spectacular became the scene. There were millions of flowers—thousands and thousands of acres of them, as far as the eye could see in any direction. It was a brilliant floral quilt of white and blue and purple, yellow, orange and flaming red.

Since he and his crew were filming special-interest segments for television, they got their cameras out and went to work. Every time they saw a different variety, they stopped. But then, the sound man would walk away from the road, crest the next hill and shout, "Oh, man, come look at this one!" And the camera-man would trudge up there with the gear. The bus driver would try to keep close on the road with their bus, and then he would shout from the road, "There's a whole bunch of iris-looking things down here by the creek!" And down the hill they'd plod. Kuralt said, "I suppose we walked fifteen or twenty miles of the eighty miles to Medicine Bow that day in quest of little bits of beauty" (p. 156).

Think of all that lovely, soul-soaring beauty that few people ever see. Why did God create such beauty and diversity? Because His creation reflects Him, and like a master craftsman who does a good job regardless of whether or not anyone sees it, God did a good job even if we don't see it. Nature itself cries glory to God.

God tips His hand in creation.

Why did God create the way He did? Well, for one reason, as an artist, he reflected Himself in His art. So, in that sense, it was inescapable. On a more advanced level, we might say that God, being the source of all goodness in the world, wants people to get an accurate picture of who He is, so they will be inclined to believe in Him. God is not willing for anyone to perish, so He wants to be sure everyone understand who He is. Thus God tips His hand in creation.

In fact, in Romans 1:20 we read that since the creation of the world God's invisible attributes are clearly seen, being understood by the things that are created. The result, as the apostle Paul goes on to write, is that anyone who rejects God is without excuse because of what they have seen of Him in nature.

Conclusion

So, in summary, what did God have in mind when He created? He had in mind to create a beautiful world that reflected His attributes. In that beautiful world, He intended to create humanity, a class of created beings with whom He could be friends, with whom He could fellowship, with whom He could share His glory, and to whom He could reveal His kindness forever. This was to bring glory to Him as creator, but not a selfish glory—a loving, sharing glory.

That original intention was destroyed by sin in the garden of Eden. Now God is in the process of restoring that intention with a new heaven and a new earth and a family of children that have been born again spiritually, and are worthy, through Christ, of sharing heaven with the triune God forever.

Speed Bump

Slow down to be sure you've gotten the main points from this chapter.

Question
Answer

Q1. Why did God create in the first place?

A1. God created to reveal His *glory*.

Q2. Why did God create humanity as He did?

A2. God intended to populate the world with people with whom He could *share* His love and reveal His glory forever.

Q3. Why did God create the world as He did?

A3. God intended the world to *reflect* His character and His glory.

Fill in the Blank

Question
Answer

Q1. Why did God create in the first place?

A1. God created to reveal His _____.

Q2. Why did God create humanity as He did?

A2. God intended to populate the world with people with whom He could _____ His love and reveal His glory forever.

Q3. Why did God create the world as He did?

A3. God intended the world to _____ His character and His glory.

For Further Thought and Discussion

1. Has it ever bothered you when you heard that God created the world to reveal His glory? Did you know that He intended all along to share His glory with His children? How does this information change your concept of God and creation?

2. Had you ever thought about God creating us because He wanted us to be His friends? What do you think of that? How do you reconcile that idea with the fact that God allows His children to suffer? Do you think God has failed in His friendship? How does God sustain His friendship with us even when He allows us to suffer?

3. What is the most beautiful thing you have ever seen in nature? What insight can that sight give you into who God is?

What If I Don't Believe?

If I don't believe that God created for His glory, but that He deserves the glory because everything good and great about Him is true, I might be deceived into thinking that God's motives in creating were less than noble. In addition, I would fail to recognize that He intends to share His glory with us, and confer His glory to us.

For Further Study

1. Scripture

- Psalm 19:1
- Isaiah 43:7
- John 3:16
- John 15:15
- Romans 8:15–16, 18
- 1 Corinthians 2:7
- Ephesians 5:25–27
- 1 John 4:8
- Revelation 4:11
- Revelation 5:13

2. Books

Desiring God, John Piper
How Should We Then Live? Francis Schaeffer
What's So Amazing About Grace? Philip Yancey

There is no minor sin when God's justice confronts you,
And no major sin when His grace confronts you.
■ Anonymous

What Went Wrong with Creation?

Dr. Karl Menninger, the renowned psychiatrist, wrote one time of a stern-faced, plainly dressed man who was standing on a street corner of the Chicago Loop (the very heart of downtown Chicago). As people hurried by on their way to lunch or business, the man would solemnly lift his right arm, point to the nearest passing person, and shout, "GUILTY!" Then, without any change of expression, he would resume his stiff stance for a short time before doing it again. Then, in obedience to some apparent internal cue, he would raise the arm again, point to another hapless passerby and moan, "GUILTY!"

The effect this had on people was dramatic. They stared at him, looked at their friends, looked at him again, and hurried away. When the proclaimer of guilt pointed his finger at one man and intoned loudly, "GUILTY," the man he pointed to turned to a friend and exclaimed, "But how did *he* know?"

In this chapter we learn that . . .

1. Sin is anything that does not conform to or that transgresses the will of God.
2. Adam and Eve sinned because they believed Satan's lie that there was something better to life than what God was giving them.
3. The effect of sin is our alienation from God, from others, from ourselves, and from the created world.

I guess he knew because, odd as he was, he seemed to have grasped one basic truth: we are all guilty of something.

I read one time of a woman who was repairing a gilded picture frame, and she needed some more gilt (gold paint) to complete the repair. She went to a specialty hardware store and asked the clerk behind the counter if she had any gilt. The clerk replied, "Oh, yes. Sometimes its almost unbearable!"

Indeed, each of us is guilty! We have fallen short of God's requirements (Romans 3:23). Sometimes we feel the weight of it, and sometimes we don't. But regardless, we all stand condemned before God.

So, what went wrong? If God had in mind creating a paradise and populating it with people whom He could love and by whom He could be loved, what went wrong?

The answer: sin.

Sin is what went wrong with creation. But why? And how? And what is the consequence?

What Is Sin?

Sin is anything that does not conform to or that transgresses the will of God.

It is very difficult to define sin. It has more than one meaning. For example, one expression of sin is that it is a transgression, a going beyond the bounds, coloring outside the lines, doing something you shouldn't do. Another expression of sin is a missing of the mark, a falling short, a failure to live up to expectations. There are other words for sin that mean "lawlessness," "debt," and "ungodliness." So any definition of sin must be broad enough to allow these expressions of sin to fit under it.

St. Augustine described sin as turning away from the "universal" to the "individual" part. He taught that there was nothing more important, more desirable, more worthy than the whole. So, when someone desires something other than the whole, he, himself, grows smaller.

Having said this, there is an important distinction we must make. We are not sinners because we sin. Rather, we sin because we are sinners. That is, we are born with an inability not to sin. Our spirits, our characters are flawed. Certainly, we are capable of doing good, but we are also incapable of not doing bad.

So, we sin because we are bent to sin, and the consequences of our sin are calamitous. Cornelius Plantinga, in his book *Not the Way It's Supposed to Be*, has written of sin in relationship to the concept of shalom:

The webbing together of God, humans, and all creation in justice, fulfillment, and delight is what the Hebrew prophets call *shalom*. We call it peace, but it means far more than mere peace of mind or a ceasefire between enemies. In the Bible, shalom means universal flourishing, wholeness, and delight—a rich state of affairs in which natural needs are satisfied and natural gifts fruitfully employed, a state of affairs that inspires joyful wonder as its Creator and Savior opens doors and welcomes the creatures in whom he delights. Shalom, in other words, is the way things ought to be. (10)

Once we understand the concept of shalom, Plantinga's concept of sin can be introduced:

God is . . . not arbitrarily offended. God hates sin not just because it violates his law but, more substantively, because it violates shalom, because it breaks the peace, because it interferes with the way things are supposed to be. (Indeed, that is why God has laws against a good deal of sin.) God is for shalom, and therefore against sin. In fact, we may safely describe evil as any spoiling of shalom, whether physically (e.g., by disease), morally, spiritually, or otherwise. Moral and spiritual evil are agential evil—that is, evil that, roughly speaking, only persons can do or have. Agential evil thus comprises evil acts and dispositions. Sin, then, is any . . . evil for which some person (or groups of persons) is to blame. In short, sin is culpable (deserving blame) shalom-breaking. (14)

We see, then, that sin is a multifaceted thing. Many things can be said of sin, and all of them are true, which makes it difficult to define. But anything other than what God wants is sin, whether it is something forbidden that we did, or something commanded that we didn't do, or any other negative effect on God's creation.

Why Did Adam and Eve Sin?

Adam and Eve sinned because they believed Satan's lie that there was something better to life than what God was giving them.

Where did sin come from? Why did God create something that was corruptible? Why did Adam and Eve sin? And how has it affected us?

The answers to these questions fade into mystery in many places. We are simply not given enough information in the Bible to have a clear answer for them all. However, we can put two and two together and come up with some insights that help us.

First, we do not know where sin came from. God did not sin, nor create sin, nor can He be blamed for sin. God's character is perfect. Francis Schaeffer said that God created the "potentiality" of evil, but not the "actuality" of it.

It was angels and humans who sinned. In Deuteronomy 32:4, we read, "His work is perfect; for all his ways are justice. A God of faithfulness and without iniquity, just and right is he" (RSV). In Job 34:10 we read, "Far be it from God that he should do wickedness, and from the Almighty that he should do wrong" (RSV). And in James 1:13, we read that it is impossible for God even to desire to do wrong: "God cannot be tempted with evil and he himself tempts no one" (RSV). So God is not responsible for sin.

Why I Need to Know This

I need to know this because otherwise I might not take my sin seriously enough. I need to know that I have sinned, and that this sin has terrible consequences.

Yet, on the other hand, we must not say that there is an eternal, evil power in the universe equal to God Himself. This idea is called "dualism," meaning the existence of two equally ultimate powers, one good and the other evil. Sin did not surprise God. Nor can we deny that God, of His own perfect and free will, created a world in which sin was possible, through the voluntary moral choices of His moral creatures. But we cannot attribute wrong to God. The Bible doesn't give us that option.

So where did sin come from? Well, Adam and Eve were tempted by the devil. Sin was already found in him.

Why did the devil sin? The Bible only tells us that he wanted to be like God, to raise himself up to be on the same level as God. It does not tell us why Satan was not content to be a favored angel living in the presence of God. We only know that he wasn't. And he **In retrospect, sin makes no sense.** lied to Adam and Eve in the Garden, deceiving them into thinking that there was more that they could have than what God was giving them.

This makes no sense, of course, in retrospect. Perhaps Adam and Eve slapped their foreheads many times in their later years, not able to believe they were so easily duped. They were the pinnacle of God's creation, the apple of His eye. He put them in paradise and communed with them face to face. It was a seemingly perfect situation. But Satan came along and said, "Has God indeed said that you shall not eat of every tree in the garden?" And Eve replied that they could eat of any tree except the tree of the knowledge of good and evil. If they did, they would die.

The snake said, "You will not surely die." (Liar!) "God knows that if you eat of that tree, you will be like God." (Oh, no they won't!) So doubt was planted in Eve's mind: perhaps God had not given them everything they needed to be happy. So she looked at the fruit again. (Hmmm.) She saw that it was desirable to make one wise. (Uh-oh!) She took it. She ate it. (Aaaaauu-uggghhh!)

Then she gave some to her husband. He ate it.

It was all over.

Paradise was lost.

We simply don't know why they ate. We don't know, if they were without sin, and if they had everything they wanted in paradise, and if they walked and talked face to face with God, why they were not satisfied. It seems so irrational. All sin is irrational. It made no sense for Satan to rebel against God. It made no sense for Adam and Eve to rebel against God. These were foolish choices. Though people sometimes pretend to have good reasons for sinning, when examined in the light of reality, sin ultimately doesn't make any sense. Besides being an affront to God, it is self-destructive. The shortest distance between us and the life we long for is total obedience to God. So why did they sin?

Theologians and Bible scholars have debated this issue endlessly, but no one really knows. All we know is that God is all good and all powerful. And through Adam and Eve's rebellion against God's revealed word, sin entered the world (Genesis 3:1–19). The rest is mystery. When God created us, He gave us the ability to choose between good and evil. Of this ability, C.S. Lewis wrote:

> That means creatures . . . can go either wrong or right. Some people think they can imagine a creature which was free but had no possibility of going wrong; I cannot. If a thing is free to be good it is also free to be bad. And free will is what has made evil possible. Why, then, did God give [Adam and Eve] free will? Because free will, though it makes evil possible, is also the only thing that makes possible any love or goodness or joy worth having. A world of . . . crea-

tures that worked like machines . . . would hardly be worth creating. The happiness which God designs for His higher creatures is the happiness of being freely, voluntarily united to Him and to each other in an ecstasy of love and delight compared with which the most rapturous love between a man and a woman on this earth is mere milk and water. And for that they must be free. . . .

If God thinks this state of war in the universe is a price worth paying for free will—that is, for making a live world in which creatures can do real good or harm and something of real importance can happen, instead of a toy world which only moves when He pulls the strings—then we may take it it is worth paying. (*Mere Christianity* 52–53)

But we should not fear mystery. It is only logical that finite minds would not be capable of grasping totally the infinite mind.

What Was the Effect of Sin?

The effect of sin is our alienation from God, from others, from ourselves, and from the created world.

When Adam and Eve sinned, they died, spiritually, and began to die, physically. However, not only was Adam guilty because of what he did, all of us became guilty. And not only did Adam die spiritually, but all of us died spiritually. The apostle Paul wrote, in Romans 5:18–19:

Then as one man's [Adam's] trespass led to condemnation for all men, so one man's [Jesus'] act of righteousness leads to acquittal and life for all men. For as by one man's disobedience many were made sinners, so by one man's obedience many will be made righteous [RSV].

So the Fall affected not only Adam and Eve, but all of us. After Adam and Eve ate of the tree of the knowledge of good and evil, they heard the sound of the Lord God walking in the garden in the cool of the day, and Adam and Eve hid. They were immediately alienated from God. As God announced the curse they had brought on themselves, they discovered they were alienated from each other. God said of Eve, "Your desire shall be for your husband, and he shall rule over you" (Genesis 3:16). They were alienated from themselves in that they no longer had confidence in who they were. When asked how they knew they were naked, they each passed the buck, uncomfortable with themselves and the decisions they had made. Adam said, "Eve made me do it." Eve said, "The snake made me do it." They also were alienated from the created world. The ground was cursed. Adam would work to make a living from the ground, but he would struggle against thorns and thistles, and he would only have success by the sweat of his face.

This alienation creates devastating consequences as humanity tries to cope with it. Scripture does not directly teach this, but

Alienation was a consequence of sin.

I think that humanity, having been created *by* God *for* God, only senses its worth when properly related to God. However, having cut themselves off from God, humans are now destined to try to establish self-worth by imitating God. God is sovereign, and now humanity tries to become sovereign, at least over itself. Thus control becomes the great issue. Humanity now tries to dominate four things.

1. We want to dominate God. Instead of wanting to serve God as we were created to do, we want to dominate Him. This is seen in many subtle ways. We want God to answer our prayers. We put our heavenly prayer coin in the Great Heavenly Vending Machine, and we expect to get our answer out. When we don't get it, we kick the door and slam the coin return and scream, "Where's our answer?"

We want Him to make our lives peaceful and prosperous. We want Him to use His power to give us good jobs and good homes and good spouses and good children and good health and good friends and a good, long life, and a good, easy death. When He doesn't, we yell, "Why me?"

We want Him to make the suffering in the world go away. We want Him to punish evil and reward good in this life. We want Him to give us sunshine when we have picnics, and rain when we plant our gardens. We want, we want, we want. When we don't get, we cry, "Why do bad things happen to good people?"

We would never be so bold as to say that we want God to bow down to us. We just want Him to do what we want Him to do, and we don't see that the two are the same.

Probably the number one reason people say that they don't believe in God is that they don't understand why bad things happen to good people. They don't understand why the innocent suffer. A news commentator, after hearing a little girl who had suffered terribly still voice her faith in God, said, "I admire the faith of a little girl who gives God the credit for all the good in the world, but doesn't blame Him for all the evil."

We want to dominate God. The problem is, we cannot dominate Him. He will not be dominated. He will not fit into our box. He will not answer to our beck and call. When we rub His **The drive to dominate is an effort to imitate God.** bottle, He will not pop out and grant us three wishes. So we get angry with God. We fight with Him. We resent Him. We reject Him. Or we just ignore Him, which is passive rebellion.

2. We want to dominate others. Instead of wanting to serve others as we were created to do, we want to dominate them. The essence of relationships within the Trinity is a mutual submission. Each member of the Trinity lives in total fellowship and harmony with the others.

Humanity has been created in God's image, and as such, we can only expect fellowship and harmony when we live in mutual submission to one another. Jesus said that if we love God with all our hearts, and love our neighbors as ourselves, we fulfill all the law and the prophets (Matthew 22:39–41). He also said, "Do unto others as you would have others do unto you" (Matthew 7:12). The apostle Paul said of husband/wife, parent/child, and master/slave relationships that they were all founded on the principle of being subject to one another (Ephesians 5:22—6:9). The one in authority is subject to the needs of those under him, and those under authority are subject to the authority of those over them. In this way, all people get their needs met in a context of unity and harmony.

All this has been turned around. We do not naturally submit to one another. We do not naturally do unto others as we would have others do unto us. We do not naturally love God and our neighbors as ourselves. Rather we want to dominate them. We want our spouse to love us. We want our children to obey us. We want our employer to treat **Submission goes** us with respect, which by itself is not wrong. **against our nature.** But when they don't, rather than to continue to love them in return, how often do we hide or hurt? How often do we retaliate or retreat? How many marriages do you know that are true models of selfless love? How many parent/child relationships? How many employer/employee relationships?

I feel the pull myself. When my wife doesn't meet my expectations, I have been known to speak unkindly or withdraw in silence. How would I like it if God treated me the way I treat my spouse or my child or my employer or employee or neighbor? If we hope that God will love us unconditionally, why do we feel that we can do less to others?

Yet, that is what happened at the Fall. We were given an inordinate desire to dominate others. And that is what accounts for most of the pain, evil, and suffering in the world. That is the reason for war, for the Inquisition, for the Crusades, for economic oppression, for slavery, for discrimination of every sort. It is a great and profound evil.

Complicating this illicit desire is the fact that we cannot dominate others. We cannot get others to do what we want them to. Oh, we may have some influence over others, but not the degree that we want. The communists could not control their subjects, the politicians cannot control their voters, parents cannot control their children, and employees cannot control their bosses. So they get angry, resentful, bitter, or depressed.

3. We want to dominate ourselves. This is a very difficult trick. We want to be self-disciplined. We want to weigh the right weight, have the right hair, have the right face, have the right talents, have the right attitude, have the right memory, have the right wisdom and insight. We want to be able to do what we want to do, but our desires always exceed our ability. We cannot achieve perfection. We cannot control even ourselves.

As a result, we wrestle with self-contempt, with poor self-images, with feelings of inferiority, insecurity, and inadequacy. We try to cover it up by friends we gain, or possessions we gain, or success we gain. But we can never gain enough to erase the nagging doubts about our inherent self-worth. Cut loose from God, we never quite recover.

We cannot control even ourselves.

4. We want to control creation. We want crops to grow. We want to find gold and silver and iron and copper. We want to cut down trees to make money. We want to dam up rivers to create cities in the desert. We want to build factories and nuclear power plants. We want to build subdivisions. We want to drive to many places and fly to far-off places. We want to buy and sell and make money, and we want creation to yield its resources to help our cause.

At the same time, we want wilderness areas, and clean water, and clean air, and beautiful vistas, and healthy plant life. But we have not been careful enough or willing enough to pay the price to keep creation clean and healthy while at the same time using the resources of the globe.

Today, we are looking at serious pollution, dwindling resources, and ecological imbalance as the earth is stripped of resources. The problems are menacing and difficult. Our desire to dominate creation was greater than our sensitivity to it, and we have ended up fouling our own nest.

We want to dominate creation, but we can't. We can only cooperate with creation. We must treat creation with respect or we will kill it, and it will in turn kill us.

Conclusion

What went wrong with creation? Sin went wrong. Adam and Eve, as representatives for all of us, sinned and brought guilt and corruption to the human race so that, while we are capable of doing good, we are incapable of not doing bad. And, we are unable to fix ourselves. Like a windowpane, we have been cracked, and there is no way to un-crack us.

We are in desperate need. We need to be reconciled to God. We need to be reconciled to each other. We need to be reconciled to ourselves. And, we need to be reconciled to God's creation. This all-important set of needs, then, sets the stage for the next chapter dealing with how God has chosen to fix what we have broken.

Speed Bump

Slow down to be sure you've gotten the main points from this chapter.

Question
Answer

Q1. What is sin?

A1. Sin is anything that does not conform to or that transgresses the *will* of God.

Q2. Why did Adam and Eve sin?

A2. Adam and Eve sinned because they believed Satan's *lie* that there was something better to life than what God was giving them.

Q3. What was the effect of sin?

A3. The effect of sin is our *alienation* from God, from others, from ourselves, and from the created world.

Fill in the Blank

*Q*uestion   **Q1.** What is sin?

*A*nswer   **A1.** Sin is anything that does not conform to or that transgresses the _____ of God.

Q2. Why did Adam and Eve sin?

A2. Adam and Eve sinned because they believed Satan's _____ that there was something better to life than what God was giving them.

Q3. What was the effect of sin?

A3. The effect of sin is our _____ from God, from others, from ourselves, and from the created world.

For Further Thought and Discussion

1. If sin is anything that does not conform to the will of God, how extensive do you think sin is in your life? Discounting the obvious things, such as lying, cheating, stealing, and murder as being sin, what other less obvious things are common in Americans' lives that would have to be considered sin under this definition?

2. Think of some excuses you have used for sins you have committed. How much sense do they make to you now?

3. What are examples you have experienced or witnessed of the alienation that exists between us and God, others, self, and creation?

What If I Don't Believe?

If I don't believe, I may deceive myself into thinking that my sin is not so bad—that I am not alienated from God, and that therefore, I don't need to be saved. If I come to this conclusion, I may ignore God's warning that I am alienated from Him and need to be saved and may miss His solution: salvation by grace through faith in Jesus.

For Further Study

1. Scripture

- Genesis 3:1–19
- Deuteronomy 32:4
- Job 34:10
- Romans 5:18–19
- James 1:13
- 1 John 1:8–10

2. Books
Some other books that would be helpful in studying this subject further are listed below.

Know What You Believe, Paul Little

Not the Way It's Supposed to Be, Cornelius Plantinga, Jr.

4

How Has God Chosen to Fix a Broken Creation?

Sometimes when we try to fix things they don't turn out the way we expect. James Herriot, Scottish veterinarian-turned-storyteller, gives an example in his book, *Every Living Thing*. He was called to a farm to treat a horse that was suffering from urticaria, an allergic-type reaction that manifested itself in ugly, angry-looking raised spots all over the horse's skin. It was not a serious condition, but very uncomfortable for the horse. When he arrived at the farm, the farmer led the horse outside the barn into the yard. It was a magnificent Shire draft horse, huge, with feet the size of dinner platters and a noble head that it tossed proudly as it pranced toward him. The horse radiated health and strength.

Antihistamines were just coming into use at that time. Herriot thought this would be an opportunity to effect a spectacular cure and impress the farmer, since the urticaria was a textbook condition for the new antihistamines. Herriot injected him with the certain fix, then stood back to witness his impressive cure. The antihistamine would take a little while to work, and since everything seemed to be going as expected, Herriot turned to leave. As he did, the farmer said, "He's dothering a bit."

Herriot looked at the horse, and sure enough, there was the faintest tremor in the muscles of the limbs, almost invisible. Then, as he watched, it spread upwards, minute by minute, until the skin over the back, rump, and neck began to quiver. Then it began to increase in intensity. When the farmer asked what it was, Herriot passed it off as just a little reaction.

However, with agonizing slowness, the trembling progressed into an unmistakable shaking of the entire body, steadily increasing in violence. Finally, the horse was racked with convulsions. Foam began to drip from its mouth. Herriot couldn't believe what he was seeing. There was absolutely nothing he had done that could have caused this reaction, yet here it was. His heart began to pound and his mouth went dry. Surely this couldn't continue. Surely it would get better soon.

I was wrong. Almost imperceptibly the huge animal began to sway. Only a little bit at first, then more and more till he was tilting from side to side like a mighty oak in a gale. Oh, dear God, he was going to go down and that would be the end. And that end had to come soon. The cobbles shook under my feet as the great horse crashed to the ground. For a few moments he lay there, stretched on his side, his feet pedaling convulsively, then he was still.

Well, that was it. I had killed this magnificent horse. It was impossible, unbelievable, but a few minutes ago that animal had been standing there in all his strength and beauty, and I had come along with my clever new medicines and now there he was, dead.

Herriot felt cold and miserable. What could he say to the farmer? Just as he opened his mouth and took a long quavering breath to try to begin, he noticed a slight movement of the horse's head. He said nothing. Nor did the farmer, who was standing there, bug-eyed. The big animal eased himself onto his chest, looked around for a few seconds, and got to his feet. He shook his head, then walked across to the farmer. The recovery had been just as quick, just as incredible, as the horrifying collapse, and he showed no ill effects, either from the medicine or the thunderous fall. The farmer reached up and patted the horse's neck.

"You know, Mr. Herriot, them spots have nearly gone!"

I walked over and took a look. "That's right. You can hardly see them now."

[The farmer] shook his head wonderingly. "Aye, well, it's a wonderful new treatment, but I'll tell you something. I hope you don't mind me sayin' this, but"—he put his hand on my arm and looked up into my face—"I think it's just a bit drastic."

And so it is; when we try to fix things, they don't always turn out the way we expect. Even when God fixes things, they don't always turn out the way *we* expect. That is not to say they turn out wrong. It's just that they don't always turn out the way we expect. Just as Herriot's antihistamine eventually fixed the horse, so God's intervention eventually fixes the problem with creation. But it does not all happen as we might have anticipated.

In this chapter we learn that . . .

1. God responded to the Fall by saving those who truly believed Him.
2. God chose Israel as His special people through whom to bring salvation to all the other nations of the world.
3. Jesus came in fulfillment of God's promises to Israel, including the broadening of His covenant to include Gentiles.

God created a perfect paradise and populated it with humanity, with whom He wanted a genuine friendship. But then, without warning, sin entered paradise, spoiling God's original design. Next, contrary to what one might have expected, God chose to restore His creation, rather than merely destroy it.

How Did God Respond to the Fall of Humanity?

God responded to the Fall by saving those who truly believed Him.

God's grace went into immediate action with the fall of Adam and Eve, to reclaim and restore them from sin. And His spirit of "rescue" has been extended to all humanity since. The first thing God did was make clothing for them from animal skin to cover them, because they knew they were naked. This was a sign of His first act of redemption. Some have speculated that the killing of the animals from which God got the skins was the first animal sacrifice to atone for Adam and Eve's sin.

In addition, God promised deliverance through one of Adam and Eve's descendants. In the curse of the serpent in Genesis 3:15, we read, "And I will put enmity between you and the woman, and between your seed and her Seed [meaning Jesus]; He shall bruise your head and you shall bruise His heel."

The bruising of the heel of Eve's seed is understood to be the crucifixion (the bruising of the heel, while painful, is not fatal), while the bruising of the head of Satan is understood to be Christ's ultimate triumph over Satan (the bruising of the head is understood to be fatal).

This approach of God is seen throughout the Bible. He is constantly implementing His plan to redeem and save those who will respond with obedient faith. He promises to restore and bless humanity if humanity will believe in Him and follow Him. Yet, humanity seems bent on rejecting Him. Adam and Eve's descendants increased in numbers and inclination to sin until, at one time, God looked down upon the earth and there were only eight people who were willing to live in a righteous relationship with Him: Noah and his immediate family—his wife, his three sons, and their wives. So God performed, as it were, surgery on the human race, cutting away the cancerous tissue and leaving behind the healthy tissue to grow and restore itself. He destroyed all humanity with the Great Flood, but saved Noah and his family in the ark (Genesis 6—8).

God then commissioned Noah and his family to be fruitful and multiply and fill the earth. However, as Noah's descendants began to multiply in numbers, so their inclination to sin also multiplied. They began building the Tower of Babel, a colossal monument to themselves, so that the memory of their people would never disappear from the face of the earth. God did not want them to build the tower. It was symbolic of humanity's desire to share the power and glory that belong only to God. So God confused their languages so that they could no longer understand each other and cooperate on this common project.

So, the history of humanity to this point is a history of rejecting God. He tried to offer redemption to all humanity, He tried to restore humanity when it went astray, yet nothing worked. The Tower of Babel was the greatest affront to God yet—not an individual or a clan rebelling, but all the people organized in sophisticated civilization scheming and building without thought of God (Genesis 11:1–9). So what was God to do with this rebellious creation? The sinfulness of humanity deepened and broadened in its effects, and God's judgments mixed with His mercy did not solve the problem.

Why I Need to Know This

I need to know this so that I can understand that God's first impulse when His creation was corrupted by the presence of sin was to restore it. When I see His instantaneous and continuous efforts to regain that which was lost, I get insight into His love and desire for my fellowship.

Why Did God Choose Israel?

God chose Israel as His special people through whom to bring salvation to all the other nations of the world.

With the judgment at Babel, scattering humanity throughout the earth with many languages, cultures, and barriers to easy unity, we recognize the world that we inhabit today: Genesis 3—11 show that sin is universal, an "equal opportunity" destroyer. The end of Genesis 11 implies a key question: What will God do now? The answer comes unexpectedly and is expressed in a whimsical couplet by the poet and playwright Archibald Macleish:

> How odd of God
> To choose the Jews.

The loving, rescuing, and restoring God did not abandon humanity after it proved itself unfailingly rebellious. Instead He chose one family, Abraham's (whose descendants were later called "Jews"). With Abraham's call, God's drama of redemption, what theologians call "salvation history," gets fully underway.

The calling of Abraham and, through him, of ancient Israel, discloses God's way of saving fallen humanity:

1. God chose Israel as His special nation of worshipers, of representatives of Him to the world, of recipients of His blessing (Exodus 19:5–6).
2. As Israel obeyed God, the blessings of the nation would be seen by other nations, not merely as good luck or effective leadership, but as the clear hand of God's blessing.
3. As other nations see God's self-revelation, through His work and blessing on the nation of Israel, they would want to know Him because of what they saw of Him in Israel.

About a thousand years after Abraham, during David's reign and the first part of Solomon's reign, Israel experienced its most prolonged period of righteousness, and God blessed mightily. Militarily, they were undefeatable. Economically, they were wealthy. Socially, they had peace, stability, and strong cultural growth. They were the envy of the world.

In fact, the queen of Sheba heard about the wisdom and wealth of Solomon in the early part of his reign and could not believe what she heard. So she decided to visit him (1 Kings 10). Solomon answered her questions, showed her his buildings and the temple. When she saw it all, she swooned ("There was no more spirit in her," v. 5). Then she broke out in a spontaneous eulogy to God: "Blessed be the Lord your God, who delighted in you, setting you on the throne of Israel. Because the Lord has loved Israel forever, therefore He made you king, to do justice and righteousness" (v. 9).

This is as it was supposed to work. As David wrote in Psalm 67:

> God be merciful to us and bless us,
> And cause His face to shine upon us.
> Selah
> That Your way may be known on earth,
> Your salvation among all nations.
> God shall bless us,
> And all the ends of the earth shall fear Him (vv. 1, 7).

God's blessing on the nation of Israel resulted in other nations fearing Him.

The centerpieces of God's dealings with Israel are three covenants, binding agreements including promises to be fulfilled later. Two covenants were unconditional—that is, God promised to bless Israel without any reciprocation required from Israel—and one was conditional—that is, dependent upon Israel's response.

The Abrahamic Covenant. The first covenant was the Abrahamic Covenant, found in Genesis 12:1–3, in which God promised to bless Abraham in three areas: (1) national—God promised to give Abraham a permanent land in which He would make a great nation out of his descendants; (2) personal—God promised to bless Abraham personally, making his name great and blessing those who blessed Abraham; and (3) universal—God promised to bless the whole world through Abraham, which pointed to Jesus, the Messiah, who would offer salvation to the whole world.

God has worked consistently in fulfilling His unilateral covenant with Abraham. Regarding the first part of the covenant, He gave Abraham's descendants a land and nation. Some be-

God's agreement with Abraham was unconditional.

lieve the covenant has already been totally fulfilled, and others believe it has been only partially fulfilled, with complete fulfillment to occur in the future, after the return of Christ. Regarding the second part, Abraham was indeed blessed personally by God in His lifetime. And finally, the Messiah has come and is in the process of fulfilling the final part of the covenant, and will continue until He returns.

The Mosaic Covenant. The second major covenant God made with Israel was the Mosaic Covenant, or the Law, and it is conditional. That is, the blessings of the Law depend on Israel's obedience to it. This covenant was given to the nation of Israel so that those who were given the Abrahamic Covenant would know how to conduct themselves.

There are three parts to this covenant. First was the moral law, which governed how the Israelites were to conduct themselves personally before God and with each other. The Ten Commandments are central to this part of the covenant, and embody moral behavior (Exodus 20:1–26). The second was the civil law, which outlined how the Israelites would govern themselves as a nation, and how they would relate socially with each other (Exodus 21:1—24:11). The third was the ceremonial law, which governed their religious lives and outlined how they should relate to God, and how they should approach Him on the strict conditions that He laid down (Exodus 24:12—31:18).

Much about the Mosaic Law was symbolic. It was given to a people who were slaves. They were led out of slavery in Egypt and taken to Mt. Sinai, where they were given the Law. The symbolism is inescapable: as they were freed from physical slavery by the Exodus, so they could be freed from spiritual slavery by the Law. Now, having saved them, God makes a covenant with them, which involves giving them the Law of Moses to live by.

Many people look at the Law and think that it must have been a great burden. There were many laws, governing everything from how and what to eat, to what to do if you find your

The Law was a source of freedom, not slavery. neighbor's lost animal, to how to rear your children. However, the burden of righteousness is nowhere near as heavy as the burden of unrighteousness. The Law saved people from the cause/effect consequences of sin and brought a person into harmony with God, with himself, and with other people. The Law was not a source of slavery but a source of freedom. David wrote, in Psalm 19:7–11:

> The law of the LORD is perfect,
>   converting the soul;
> The testimony of the LORD is sure,
>   making wise the simple;
> The statutes of the LORD are right,
>   rejoicing the heart;
> The commandment of the LORD is pure,
>   enlightening the eyes;
> The fear of the LORD is clean,
>   enduring forever;
> The judgments of the LORD are true
>   and righteous altogether.
> More to be desired are they than gold,
> Yea, than much fine gold;
> Sweeter also than honey and the
>   honeycomb.
> Moreover by them Your servant is
>   warned,
> And in keeping them there is great
>   reward.

This is not the picture of something burdensome, constraining, and foreboding. Rather it is the picture of something helpful, freeing, and desirable. It is described as pleasant, desirable, and profitable. This impression is reinforced in Psalm 1:1–3:

> Blessed is the man
> Who walks not in the counsel of the
> ungodly,
> Nor stands in the path of sinners,
> Nor sits in the seat of the scornful;
> But his delight is in the law of the
>   LORD
> And in His law he meditates day and
>   night.
> He shall be like a tree
> Planted by the rivers of water,
> That brings forth its fruit in its
>   season,
> Whose leaf also shall not wither;
> And whatever he does shall prosper.

Again, the picture of the Mosaic Law here is not one of grimace, grin and bear it, but of rich blessing for joyful obedience. Who wouldn't want to be fruitful and prosper in whatever he does?

The Mosaic Covenant did not replace the Abrahamic Covenant, but rather built upon it. The Abrahamic Covenant identified Israel as the covenant people of God, while the Mosaic Covenant outlined how this covenant people should live, before God and with each other. It was not given so that by keeping the Law people could be saved. Rather it was given so that, if they were saved and wanted to live a life pleasing to God and constructive for themselves, they would know how to do it. However, as people tried to keep the Law, it became evident that it was impossible. The result was a vivid demonstration that no one can possibly keep all the Law, and one's only hope of righteousness was through the mercy and grace of God.

The New Covenant. After the failure of Israel to live up to the Mosaic Covenant, God offered the third major covenant, the New Covenant, found in Jeremiah 31–34, in which God promised two critical things: (1) to write His law on their hearts (31:33) rather than only on tablets of stone; and (2) to bring Israel into a personal knowledge of Him and to forgive their sin (31:34). Having demonstrated through the Mosaic Covenant that humanity cannot be faithful with the law written on tablets of stone, God promised to write the law on the tablets of their heart, which is apparently a reference to the indwelling Holy Spirit and the new birth which result from faith in Christ. The New Covenant is made possible by the death and resurrection of Jesus, who offers spiritual rebirth and forgiveness of sin in return for believing in and receiving Him (John 1:12).

God seems to delight in giving blessings. God seems to delight in being a covenant maker and a covenant keeper. He seems to delight in promising blessing and then giving it. He seems to long for humanity to respond to Him in faith and obedience. The covenants form the framework for the entire program of God in the world.

Yet, Israel did not perform well under the Mosaic Covenant, the "conditional" covenant. In spite of the obvious link between obedience and blessing that was demonstrated from king to king, nevertheless the nation persisted in unbelief and disobedience. The Old Testament prophets thundered warnings of curses and calamities if the nation did not repent and return to God, but there was a downward march of spiritual life in Israel that was as certain and ominous as an executioner descending the stairs to his dungeon. God acknowledged that the covenants were not working, that the people were too weak-willed, too sinful to fulfill their part of the Mosaic Covenant. With the covenant consistently and flagrantly broken, the question arises, "What is God going to do?"

From God's point of view, we have to ask, "What more could He do?" He poured out staggering blessing on the nation of Israel, and they spit in His face. Take Solomon as an example. When God asked the promising young king what he would like to receive from God, Solomon did not ask for wealth, health, long life, or peace from his enemies. He asked for wisdom to lead the great nation of God. His request was granted. His wisdom was legendary. Yet by the end of his life, Solomon had multiple foreign wives to himself in violation of the Mosaic Law, and in the end he was worshiping their gods, in spite of God's direct revelation and profound temporal blessing on his life. Humanity seems unable to sustain peace and prosperity. We seem bent to take credit for all blessing, and blame God for all misfortune.

Time and again, God sent prophets to call the nation to repentance, and there were episodes of a returning to God under certain **God warned the people repeatedly.** kings, but commonly, after one righteous king died, a son would assume the throne who would lead the Israelites into the abominable practices of the pagan religions around them.

The Hebrews violated the covenants, in ways other than their flagrant wickedness in turning from God to idols. They also distorted the features of the covenant in godless, self-centered ways that seemed good on the surface. For example, in the prophet Jeremiah's time the existence of the temple as God's house in Jerusalem was thought to guarantee God's continuing favor upon and protection for the city, regardless of how wicked the people were. It was an almost magical view of the temple, like a great granite "rabbit's foot" that brought good luck.

Another example later on was the legalistic Pharisees and Saducees who kept the letter of the Law but violated the spirit, and who raised man-made laws to a level higher than Scripture, so that they violated Scripture in keeping their traditions.

The angels in heaven must have sighed with heaviness to see the relentless, downward march of spiritual reality in God's people. It finally became so serious that God had no choice but to destroy the nation, since the Mosaic Covenant promised blessing for obedience but cursing for disobedience (Deuteronomy 27—28).

Why Did Jesus Come?

Jesus came in fulfillment of God's promises to Israel, including the broadening of His covenant to include Gentiles.

Jesus came to earth because He is the one in whom all three covenants are fulfilled. He fulfills God's promise to Abraham that "in you all the families of the earth shall be blessed." Through Jesus, the Messiah, all the families of the earth are blessed through Abraham, since Jesus is, through Mary, a descendant of Abraham.

Jesus is the fulfillment of the Mosaic Covenant in that He fulfilled the Law perfectly (Matthew 5—7), meeting God's requirements for faith and loving obedience. For example, when Satan tempted Jesus in the desert after forty days of fasting, Jesus withstood his temptation, whereas Adam and Eve did not. Jesus said, "Do not think that I came to destroy the Law or the Prophets. I did not come to destroy but to fulfill. For assuredly, I say to you, till heaven and earth pass away, one jot or one tittle will by no means pass from the law till all is fulfilled" (Matthew 5:18).

Finally, through Jesus God fulfills the New Covenant promises to "put My law in their minds, and write it on their hearts," and to "forgive their iniquity, and their sin I will remember no more" (Jeremiah 31:33, 34; Hebrews 8:6–13). Through Jesus we may be born again (John 3:5; Ezekiel 36:25–27), and through Jesus God forgives our sins (1 John 1:7–9).

Jesus' perfect life and perfect death open the door for God's promises to Israel to be fulfilled. Israel failed to live up to the Mosaic Covenant both by failing to keep God's most basic commandments and by failing to represent God adequately to the other nations. In His life, Jesus does both of these and in this way truly fulfills for Israel—and the whole world—all that God required of His chosen people. Jesus' life is a perfect example for us to follow in righteous living, in loving others, in suffering for the sake of the kingdom of God, and in proclaiming the message of salvation.

Jesus' perfect life and death helped God's promises to be fulfilled.

In Jesus' death, we see the Great Sacrifice that atones for sin (1

John 2:1–2; 2 Corinthians 5:18, 19; Romans 3:24–26). Each of us, as we have already seen, is guilty of the death of Christ. Certainly, it was Judas who betrayed Him, the religious leaders of Jerusalem who were responsible for having Him arrested, Pilate who was responsible for signing His death warrant, the soldiers for actually nailing Him to the cross. There is plenty of direct guilt to go around. But beyond that, each of us is guilty.

Who of us has not sinned against God and others by betraying someone for money, as Judas did, or to save our skin, as Peter did? Who has not been envious of another's influence, as the religious leaders were of Jesus, and then—in heart if not in act—sought to bring him or her down? Who has not tried to run from the responsibility of doing the right thing, as Pilate did, when we fear the displeasure of the crowd or choose an easy, but unjust, way out of a difficult situation? And who has not rationalized his failures to speak up for truth and righteousness and then soothed his conscience by saying, as the Roman soldiers may have, "I'm just doing what they told me to do"? Though separated by time, we have all been united in word, attitude, and action with those who crucified Jesus. We were there when they crucified the Lord—and we helped!

Why did Jesus come? The angel told Joseph to call Mary's child "Jesus" because He would "save His people from their sins" (Mathew 1:21). His example in living shows us how to live; but His accomplishment in dying was to atone for our sins and give us life. Jesus fulfilled the three major covenants, and they culminate in the salvation that the Messiah accomplished. The Old Testament sacrificial system pointed, as an object lesson, toward the ultimate sacrifice that Jesus made. While the blood of bulls and goats covered sin for a moment, it was not until Jesus came to die for us that the sin would actually be taken away. It was not until Jesus came to die on the cross that the Old Testament covenants would finally be fulfilled.

Conclusion

In previous chapters, we asked the questions, "What did God have in mind when He created," and "What went wrong with creation?" We answered that God had in mind a creation that would bring glory to Him and allow Him to love and be loved by humanity. What went wrong is that humanity sinned, and God's original plan was thwarted. Now in this chapter, we ask "How has God chosen to fix it?" and the answer is that He has chosen to send Christ to die for our sins so that those who believe in and receive Him as their personal savior can become forgiven children of God and be restored to their original place in God's plan. In the process, Jesus fulfilled covenants that God made with humanity, but even the covenants depended on the fundamental reason for Jesus' coming, namely, to be a substitutionary sacrifice for our sins—that is, to die in our place (to be our substitute), so that we would not have to pay the eternal penalty for our own sins.

Believers immediately gain a closer fellowship with God.

Then, in His time, reborn people will enter a renewed heaven and earth to live in splendor and glory forever. In a sentence, God has chosen to fix the sin problem by sending Jesus to die for our sins so that we could be restored to our original purpose, along with a restored creation.

Speed Bump

Slow down to be sure you've gotten the main points from this chapter.

Question **A**nswer

Q1. How did God respond to the fall of humanity?

A1. God responded to the Fall by *saving* those who truly believed Him.

Q2. Why did God choose Israel?

A2. God chose Israel as His special people through whom to bring *salvation* to all the other nations of the world.

Q3. Why did Jesus come?

A3. Jesus came in *fulfillment* of God's promises to Israel, including the broadening of His covenant to include Gentiles.

Fill in the Blank

Question **A**nswer

Q1. How did God respond to the fall of humanity?

A1. God responded to the Fall by _____ those who truly believed Him.

Q2. Why did God choose Israel?

A2. God chose Israel as His special people through whom to bring _____ to all the other nations of the world.

Q3. Why did Jesus come?

A3. Jesus came in _____ of God's promises to Israel, including the broadening of His covenant to include Gentiles.

For Further Thought and Discussion

1. Why do you think humanity has so consistently resisted God's desire to save them?

2. Which way do you think it would be easier to live for God, under the Mosaic Law, or under the grace of Christ? Why?

3. If our sin nailed Christ to the cross, how could we use that information to help us resist sin?

What If I Don't Believe?

If I don't believe that God has chosen to restore His original creation through Christ, I may not understand the centrality of the cross to my salvation. I may be deceived into thinking that God allows me to be saved some way other than through Christ.

For Further Study

1. Scripture

- Genesis 3:1–19
- Exodus 20:1–26
- Psalm 19:7–11
- Psalm 67:1, 7
- Jeremiah 31:31–34
- Luke 15:4–7

2. Books

Not the Way It's Supposed to Be, Cornelius Plantinga, Jr.
The Cross of Christ, John R.W. Stott
Knowing God, James I. Packer

> *Little faith will bring your soul to heaven;*
> *great faith will bring heaven to your soul.*
> ■ Charles Haddon Spurgeon (1843–1892)

What Must I Do to Be Saved?

People commonly go to one of two extremes regarding salvation. One is thinking that salvation can be earned. I will never forget, as a young seminary student, standing in the large central square in Mexico City watching a lady crawl on her hands and knees over hard, uneven stone pavement, toward the cathedral on the square. She was weeping and praying. Her hands and knees were beginning to bleed. Everyone walked past her unconcerned, as if she were not there. I stood and stared unself-consciously. I wanted somehow to help her, but didn't know how. Was she weeping for her sins? Was she seeking atonement and forgiveness from God?

That is what Martin Luther did five hundred years ago. Before the future leader of the Protestant Reformation ever became a Christian, he led a wild and sinful life. Then, after a close brush with death in a thunderstorm in July, 1505, he made a vow to become a monk. He tried as hard as he could to earn his righteousness before God by sinless living, but he could not do it. Out of deep frustration, he joined a monastery where he thought he could purge himself of his sin. He couldn't. He even went on a pilgrimage to a holy site and crawled up the stairs of the cathedral, hoping to purge his sins with each step up.

It is instinctive to think we have to do something to be saved. Many people assume we must earn our salvation—work hard enough, or be good enough.

In this chapter we learn that . . .

1. Repentance means "changing one's moral direction," turning away from evil.
2. Faith is believing what God has said and responding accordingly.
3. New birth is the transformation from spiritual death to spiritual life.

The other extreme is in thinking that everyone will go to heaven, regardless of how good or bad they are. This view is called "universalism" and is based on the assumption that God is too loving and kind to send anyone to hell. The primary difficulty with this position is that the Bible is full of passages that state categorically that people will go to hell. Jesus warned in Matthew 7:13–14, "Enter by the narrow gate; for wide is the gate and broad is the way that leads to destruction, and there are many who go in by it. Because narrow is the gate and difficult is the way which leads to life, and there are few who find it."

Revelation 20:15 states that "anyone not found written in the Book of Life was cast into the lake of fire."

So if it is incorrect that we can earn salvation by our good works and if it is incorrect that everyone will be saved regardless of his good or bad works, then what must we do to be saved?

What Is Repentance?

Repentance means "changing one's moral direction," turning away from evil.

Repentance is a key to salvation. It is not an option. We must change our thinking about who we are, about who God is, and about how we are going to relate to Him. C.S. Lewis once wrote,

> Fallen man is not simply an imperfect creature who needs improvement; he is a rebel who must lay down his arms. . . . This process of surrender—this movement full speed astern—is what Christians call repentance. Now repentance is no fun at all. It is something much harder than merely eating humble pie. It means unlearning all the self-conceit and self-will that we have been training ourselves into for thousands of years. It means killing part of yourself, undergoing a kind of death.

And so it is. And as such, it involves several things.

Conviction

Genuine repentance leading to salvation has some key characteristics that, if understood, will help us to recognize true repentance in ourselves and in others. First, genuine repentance involves a conviction of one's sin. That is, there is a realization that "I am a sinner." It means being persuaded, or convinced, or convicted of something. Jesus spoke of this in John 16:8–9 when He said, "And when He (the Holy Spirit) has come, He will convict the world of sin, . . . because they do not believe in Me." This means that the first step in changing one's mind about God is that he becomes persuaded that sin is sin, and therefore, wrong.

It is a monumental thing to say. The natural inclination resists it, the world denigrates it, and Satan discourages it. Some people find it almost impossible to say, "I am wrong." Yet, until a person comes to the place where he is able to admit it, he is lost.

In the very first sin, we see Adam and Eve being almost incapable of admitting responsibility for their sin. When God confronted Adam with his sin, Adam said, "THE WOMAN whom YOU gave to be with me, SHE gave me of the tree, and I ate" (emphasis added, Genesis 3:12). Adam blamed everyone but himself. First, he pointed the finger at Eve. "If she hadn't given me the confounded thing, I wouldn't have eaten it." Then, perhaps sensing that his case wasn't as strong as he would like it to be, he turns to God, and implies that it was His fault! "If You hadn't give me the woman, she wouldn't have offered me the fruit, and I wouldn't have eaten!" Then, the Lord goes to Eve (without absolving Adam, by the way), and says to the woman, "What is this you have done?" (Genesis 3:13), and Eve says, "The SERPENT deceived me, and I ate."

Why I Need to Know This

I need to know this so that I will be absolutely clear on what it means to be saved and how to be saved.

"It's not my fault!" is one of our first lines of defense. But God doesn't buy it. Today, we may excuse our sin because of genetic factors (all Irish have hot tempers), or family background (my granddad and my dad were both heavy drinkers), or biological necessity (a man's gotta do what a man's gotta do). These all have the common goal of shifting responsibility for our actions from where it belongs—on us. That is not to say these other factors don't make it more difficult not to sin. It just means that each of us stands before God alone, with no excuses.

In another example with a different outcome, David, king of Israel for forty years nearly three thousand years ago, sinned by committing adultery with Bathseba, a beautiful woman who was the wife of one of his army generals. Bathsheba became pregnant from the tryst, so to cover his tracks, David arranged her husband's death. Adultery was followed by lies followed by murder—not a pretty sight. But David was so consumed by his need to protect himself from discovery that no twinge of remorse seems to have shaken his soul.

Enter Nathan, a fearless, fire-breathing prophet. He told David a story about a rich man who owned countless sheep and a poor man who had only one pet lamb. When a traveler visited the rich man's house, the rich man took the poor man's pet lamb, killed it, and ate it (2 Samuel 12:1–4).

David was outraged! We might imagine that his face flushed. His neck veins bulged. This man, who had shown no remorse at taking the wife of his friend and general and then having him killed to cover his sin—this man who had shown no remorse at adultery, lying, and murder—now erupted like a volcano. Though he didn't realize it, David then pronounced the sentence that he, himself, deserved: "As the Lord lives, the man who has done this shall surely die!"

Each of us stands before God alone, with no excuses.

Again, we might imagine that Nathan, with nerves of steel, looked David directly in the eyes. Then he said,

> You are the man! Thus says the LORD God of Israel: "I anointed you king over Israel, and I delivered you from the hand of Saul. I gave you your master's house and your master's wives into your keeping, and gave you the house of Israel and Judah. And if that had been too little, I also would have given you much more! Why have you despised the commandment of the LORD, to do evil in His sight? You have killed Uriah the Hittite with the sword; you have taken his wife to be your wife, and have killed him with the sword of the people of Ammon" (7–9).

Then Nathan pronounced David's punishment for his terrible sin.

David, as king over Israel, an absolute monarch, could have said, "You lousy, no-good, loudmouth. You've stuck your nose into my business for the last time! GUARDS! Off with his head!"

But he didn't. Instead, he broke. He said, "I have sinned against the LORD."

Conviction of sin means more than acknowledging that you have sinned. It means accepting responsibility for it. It means accepting culpability (deserving of punishment). In an instant, David recognized he had sinned, that it was wrong, that he was responsible, and he mentally and emotionally turned away from the evil that he had done.

Apparently after this experience he wrote Psalm 51. He did not speak of weaknesses, or mistakes, or failures. He didn't point the finger at someone else. He didn't rationalize his behavior because of genetic or environmental influences. He stared God straight in the face, admitted guilt, and threw himself on His mercy.

It is a beautiful psalm, and worthy of some exposure here:

> Have mercy upon me, O God,
> According to Your lovingkindness;
> According to the multitude of Your
>   tender mercies,
> Blot out my transgressions.
> Wash me thoroughly from my iniquity,
> And cleanse me from my sin.
> For I acknowledge my transgressions,
> And my sin is always before me.
> Against You, You only, have I sinned,
> And done this evil in Your sight—
> That You may be found just when You speak,
> And blameless when You judge (1–4).

It is a wonderful model of repentance. It is a psalm that we can turn to when we sin and want to restore our fellowship with God.

Sorrow

Seeing people cry and weep over sin when they become Christians or when they experience renewal causes us to think that repentance is being sorry for your sins. That is not the whole story. Repentance comes from the Greek word *metanoeo*, which means to change one's mind. When someone changes his mind about God, it is often in a context of remorse and guilt over sin, and the process of confessing and experiencing a sense of forgiveness can often be emotional. However, the fact that the remorse and emotional release come at the same time as one's mind changes about God should not confuse the issue. "For godly sorrow produces repentance to salvation" says the apostle Paul in 2 Corinthians 7:10. And so it does. But the sorrow is not the repentance. One can be sorrowful without repenting, and one can repent without being sorrowful. Often people feel sorrow *and* repent.

I remember well the decision I made to give at least 10 percent of my income to the Lord. I was a seminary student and, I thought, very poor. By the time I paid my seminary bill, ate, and slept, I had virtually no money left over. Yet I became persuaded by a clear reading of the biblical teachings that God wanted me to give money to Him. So, in a very unemotional moment, I made the decision to begin giving money to the Lord. I changed my mind about my giving habits. I repented of robbing God (Malachi 3:8) and began giving Him money. I changed my thinking and my practice, but little emotion was involved.

I think that when one comes to realize what his sin has done to Jesus—nailing Him to the cross—sorrow will eventually come. But sorrow and repentance are two different things. Often, when a person comes to Christ, he does not have enough mental or emotional maturity to feel adequate sorrow for his actions. But he may, nevertheless, come to a point of being willing to repent of his sins. I was more worried about dying and going to hell the night I got saved than I was about the pain I had caused Jesus. Great sorrow for my sin came after I had been a Christian for a while and finally realized what I had done to Jesus.

> **Sorrow comes when one realizes what his sin has done to Jesus.**

My point in emphasizing this distinction is not to discourage or disparage emotions. If the emotions come, I think it can be good and healing. But, on the other hand, if a person is brought to a point of repentance by the Holy Spirit's convicting him of sin, but the person does not feel great emotion, he need not question the sincerity of his repentance. One can control one's will to repent, but one cannot control his emotions if they fail to come. There is no need to whip up emotions in order to meet a false idea of repentance, or to doubt the sincerity of heartfelt repentance that was not accomplished by tears and anguish.

Change

Whether one experiences great sorrow or not, the ultimate test of true repentance is whether or not he changes. There are those who say they repent, and may experience apparent remorse and sorrow, but who do not change their behavior or attitude or language. If a person claims to become a Christian, but experiences no such change, the Scripture gives that person little assurance that he is, in fact, a Christian. Where there is life, there is growth. If there is no growth, there is at least serious disease, and possibly no life.

Second Corinthians 5:17 tells us, "If anyone is in Christ, he is a new creation; old things have passed away, behold, all things have become new." This newness must manifest itself in newness of life. The apostle Paul wrote in Romans 6:4, "Therefore we were buried with Him through baptism into death, that just as Christ was

Change is an essential part of the new birth in Christ.

raised from the dead by the glory of the Father, even so we also should walk in newness of life." If we do not see that "newness of life," Scripture tells us to examine ourselves to be sure we're in the faith, because we may not be (2 Corinthians 13:5). There are those who will stand before God, claiming to be His children, pointing to good works that they have done, and the Lord will say, "Depart from me, I never knew you" (Matthew 7:23).

I do not mean to suggest that a true Christian will never sin again, nor that he will never have struggles, nor that he will never regress in his Christian experience. He will. And in Hebrews 12:5–11, we read of God's discipline for His children who live wayward lives. In fact, divine discipline is a proof that we are in fact children of God. When we persist in sin, God may spiritually spank us. So, the Scripture is not saying the Christian life is without struggles. It just says that change is part of the new birth, and if there is no change, there is no reason to be confident that there was new birth.

Forgiveness

Finally, we must accept forgiveness from God when it is offered. True repentance must keep us from carrying our guilt around with us after God has forgiven us. There is a tendency in some people, and I confess I am one of them, to remain morbid, morose, and melancholy about their sin. This did not happen to me when I was saved as a young man. That was a time of great freedom and release. But in subsequent years, as I struggled to be free from some of the attitudes, habits, and weaknesses of my pre-Christian days, I would sometimes commit a sin and then remain mired in guilt and remorse for days. Then one day, in a moment of insight that the Holy Spirit gave me—somewhere between a flash and a dawning—I was able to see why I was carrying around my guilt. I wanted to prove to God that I really was sorry for my sin. The way I proved that I took my sin seriously was to mope about it for a while. I began to see that this was wrong.

While sin may generate true sorrow and remorse, I was hanging on to mine, splashing water in its face and shaking it to keep it alive as long as I could, to prove to God my righteousness by taking my sin so seriously. In reality, it was a form of penance. I was trying to pay for part of my sin by being sorry a long time. God doesn't accept that kind of "payment," from me or anyone. Jesus pays for all our sin or none of it.

Jesus paid for all my sin.

Since I had believed in Him and received Him as my personal savior, that meant He paid for all of it, and it was a further transgression for me to try to do His job.

Realizing that gave me another form of release. Now, when I sin—and sometimes that sin is accompanied with great sorrow and remorse—I confess it, and let go of it as soon as possible. I accept the freedom that Christ offers me. True repentance brings forgiveness that brings peace.

In Billy Graham's book, *Unto the Hills,* he tells a story that Corrie ten Boom used to tell of a little girl who broke one of her mother's expensive teacups. The little girl came to her mother with the pieces of the cup in her hand and apologized tearfully. Her mother forgave her, told her not to cry anymore, and cleaned up the pieces and threw them in the trash. But the little girl was hanging on to her guilt. She went to the trash, picked out the pieces of the cup, brought them to her mother again and sobbed, "Mother, I'm so sorry that I broke your pretty cup."

That time, her mother spoke firmly to her, "Take those pieces and put them back in the trash can. Don't be silly enough to take them out again. I told you I forgave you, so don't cry anymore, and don't pick up the broken pieces anymore" (43).

We should do the same. After God has forgiven us, we should leave the broken pieces of our sin in the trash, and not pick them up again.

What Is Faith?

Faith is believing what God has said and responding accordingly.

Repentance and faith are two sides of the same coin. One will not repent if he does not believe, and if one truly believes, in the biblical meaning of the word, he will repent. Faith does not mean merely to believe information about something. It means to place one's trust in that information. The Greek word for faith is *pistis*. It is usually translated "faith" or "belief." The verb form of the word is *pisteuo*, which means "to believe." However, in John 2:24, the apostle John writes, "But Jesus did not commit Himself to them, because He knew all men." The word "commit" in this passage is the word *pisteuo*. This helps us see that to believe in a biblical sense means not only to admit to the truth of something, but to place one's confidence and trust in that truth—to commit to that truth.

The story is often told of a man who strung a tightrope across Niagara Falls and walked across it pushing a wheelbarrow. Then he asked the crowd, "Who thinks I can push a person across in the wheelbarrow?" Everyone raised his hand. Then he asked for a volunteer. No one raised his hand. If a person had had biblical faith in the tightrope walker, he would have gotten in the wheelbarrow.

This is the kind of faith that is required to be saved—faith that commits to what it believes. We are saved by grace through faith in Jesus Christ. Ephesians 2:8, 9 says, "For by grace you have been saved through faith, and that not of yourselves; it is the gift of God, not of works, lest anyone should boast."

Faith is more than just believing. In summary, faith is not merely believing the truth. James 2:19 says, "You believe that there is one God. You do well. Even the demons believe—and tremble! But do you want to know, O foolish man, that faith without works is dead?" Our faith must act. It must respond appropriately to the truth it embraces, or it is not yet biblical faith.

Two of the greatest functions of such faith are: to bring about *obedience* when we believe the *commands,* and to bring about *peace* when we believe the *promises.* Disobedience results from not believing the necessity of keeping the commands, and anxiety results from not believing the promises.

For example, the Bible makes it clear that everything God asks of us, He asks in order to give something good to us or to keep some harm from us. If we deeply believed that, then only a fool would be disobedient. Yet, when we are disobedient, it is usually because we have had a breakdown in faith. We have quit believing, if only for that moment, that obedience is not only honoring to God, but it is also in our best interest. John 15:10–11 says, "If you keep My commandments, you will abide in My love, just as I have kept My Father's commandments and abide in His love. These things I have spoken to you, that My joy may remain in you, and that your joy may be full." In this passage, the apostle John makes a direct link between obedience and joy. Faithful obedience is the only reliable road to joy.

On the other hand, when we fail to believe the promises of God, we open ourselves to anxiety. For example, if we don't believe the promises in Matthew 6:25–34, where Jesus promises to meet our physical needs on earth, we may be consumed with anxiety about finances and personal security. If we don't believe the **Joy and peace are by-products of faith.** promises of God about heaven, we may be eaten alive with anxiety about dying. If we don't believe His promises to forgive our sin and remove them from us as far as the east is from the west, we may be weighed down with anxiety and remorse over our sin.

We must obey the commandments of God to have joy. We must believe the promises of God if we are to have peace. But we will have neither if we do not believe, if we do not trust, if we do not have faith in God and His word.

What Is the New Birth?

New birth is the transformation from spiritual death to spiritual life.

When one repents and places his faith in Christ, he is born again. This is the third thing to happen at salvation. These (repentance, faith, and new birth) are all essentially simultaneous occurrences. However, those who hold to Reformed theology (Presbyterians and others) believe that faith is a gift of God, and that the person who is spiritually dead cannot believe until he is first born again by the Holy Spirit. Even with this view, repentance, faith, and the new birth are virtually simultaneous.

Others believe that Christian water baptism is the fulfillment of John 3:5 (unless one is born of water and of the Spirit, he cannot enter the kingdom of God), and therefore is essential to salvation. In this case, repentance and faith may come simultaneously, but the new birth must wait until baptism.

We certainly do not fully understand everything about the new birth, or there would not be so many differing and strongly held views about it. But when one becomes a Christian, when he is born again, there is something that happens to him spiritually. The new birth is not merely a metaphor, a figure of speech. It is something spiritual that takes place within a person. The Bible says that we were dead in our trespasses and sins (Ephesians 2:12 NASB). This means that we are spiritually dead. So when we are born again, we become spiritually alive. We are regenerated. Titus 3:5 says, "Not by works of righteousness which we have done, but according to His mercy He saved us, through the washing of regeneration and renewing of the Holy Spirit."

The Holy Spirit makes our spirit alive again.

To be regenerated means to be made new. This is done by the Holy Spirit. He causes our dead spirit to be made alive again. Jesus talked about this with Nicodemus, one of the powerful religious leaders of the day, in John chapter 3. Jesus said that in order to see the kingdom of God, one had to be born again spiritually.

While we do not fully understand it, perhaps the clearest discussion in all the Bible on this subject is found in Ephesians 2:

> And you He made alive, who were dead in trespasses and sins, in which you once walked according to the course of this world, according to the prince of the power of the air, the spirit who now works in the sons of disobedience among whom also we all once conducted ourselves in the lusts of our flesh, fulfilling the desires of the flesh and of the mind, and were by nature children of wrath, just as the others.
>
> But God, who is rich in mercy, because of His great love with which He loved us, even when we were dead in trespasses, made us alive together with Christ (by grace you have been saved), and raised us up together in the heavenly places in Christ Jesus that in the ages to come He might show the exceeding riches of His grace in His kindness toward us in Christ Jesus.
>
> For by grace you have been saved through faith, and that not of yourselves; it is the gift of God, not of works lest anyone should boast. For we are His workmanship, created in Christ Jesus for good works, which God prepared beforehand that we should walk in them (1–10).

What a marvelous passage, and what a wonderful explanation of our overwhelming need and God's even greater grace. The new birth gives us new life—eternal life. It is a supernatural work of the Holy Spirit. It gives us new power to live differently than we lived before. Life is not just a continuation of our old life with a religious dusting. Rather, there is new life there, enabling us to do that which we were not able to do before. The new birth is not the end. This is the beginning of life in Christ. This puts to death the idea that humanity is basically good and just needs education. The prevailing view today is that society is a bad influence on humanity, and that if we could educate and rebuild society, we could eliminate the problems with humanity. That is contrary to history, contrary to common sense, and contrary to the Bible.

Conclusion

We cannot save ourselves. We are lost and without hope. But God has provided a way for us to be saved. If we repent of our sins and our attitude toward Him, if we believe in Him and receive Jesus as our personal savior, we will be born again. This gives us new life in Christ, with a new relationship with God, new strength for living in this world, and solid hope in Him for the next.

Speed Bump

Slow down to be sure you've gotten the main points from this chapter.

Question
Answer

Q1. What is repentance?

A1. Repentance means *"changing* one's moral direction," turning away from evil.

Q2. What is faith?

A2. Faith is believing what God has said and *responding* accordingly.

Q3. What is the new birth?

A3. New birth is the *transformation* from spiritual death to spiritual life.

Fill in the Blank

Question   **Q1.** What is repentance?

Answer   **A1.** Repentance means "_____ one's mortal direction," turning away from evil.

Q2. What is faith?

A2. Faith is believing what God has said and _____ accordingly.

Q3. What is the new birth?

A3. New birth is the _____ from spiritual death to spiritual life.

For Further Discussion and Thought

1. Can you recall a time you experienced sorrow over a sin, but did not repent? Have you ever repented without feeling great sorrow? Is there anything in your life now for which you have not repented?

2. If faith means believing God and acting accordingly, are there any commands you are struggling to obey? Are there promises you are struggling to believe? Do you believe there is any anxiety or lack of joy in your life because of it?

3. Are you confident that you have experienced spiritual rebirth? If so, was it an event that you remember or just a gradual realization? If someone asked you, what would you tell them about being born again?

What If I Don't Believe?

If I don't believe that I need to repent, I will miss salvation, because it is a requirement. The same is true with faith. Intellectual recognition of a truth is not adequate. God wants us to give our lives to Him. If we don't, we cannot be saved. The same is true of the new birth. Unless we are born again, the Bible says, we cannot see the kingdom of God. We are born again by believing in and receiving Jesus as our savior (John 1:12). This is the core of what it means to be a Christian. If we don't believe this, we have no hope.

For Further Study

1. Scripture

- Genesis 3:12–13
- 2 Samuel 12:1–4
- Psalm 51
- John 2:24
- John 3:1–17
- John 16:8–9
- 2 Corinthians 7:10
- Ephesians 2:1–10

2. Books

How to Be Born Again, Billy Graham
Salvation: God's Amazing Plan, Millard Erickson

*I'm not what I want to be, I'm not what I'm
going to be, but thank God I'm not what I was.*
■ Anonymous

What Happens when I Am Saved?

Once upon a time, long, long ago in a land far, far away, a beautiful young girl was a slave to an evil band of thieves. Her masters lied and cheated and stole as their way of making a living. They were mean to the beautiful young girl. They made her cook their meals, gather the firewood, take care of the horses, mend their clothes and set up and take down their camp. If she didn't do what they told her to, they beat her and said ugly, cruel things to her.

She even had to lie and steal for them. Sometimes she even stole things her owners didn't tell her to steal, so she could have some money of her own. This made her feel bad, but she felt trapped and didn't know what else to do. She feared that the thieves would eventually kill her, but she could not escape because she had no place to go. She looked, acted, and thought like a thief. No one except other thieves would accept her as part of their society, and she could not survive alone. She had no hope.

One day, the leader of the band of thieves had an idea to make them very wealthy. He would have the beautiful young girl get a job at the estate of a very rich man and his wife who lived in a castle at the top of a large hill. Working on the inside, she could steal smaller things from them until that was no longer safe. Then, one night, she could let the band of thieves into the castle, where they would strip the castle of its treasures and make their escape to the ocean. There they would board a ship and sail to another land. There were hundreds of pounds of silver dinnerware, platters, candleholders, serving trays, and goblets. The thieves would melt it all down into silver bars, so the loot could not be recognized. They would be wealthy.

The girl's masters got her some new clothes, told her how to act and what to say, and sent her to the castle to ask for work. She got a job as a scullery maid, and the plan was set in motion. She began stealing little things, like a sterling silver spoon or goblet, and learned where the large pieces of silver were stored. She also kept her ears open to learn the location of the family gold and jewels. It would only be a matter of time. In their evil minds, the thieves were already counting the money as they waited for the right time to break in and loot the castle. The plan was working—they thought.

In this chapter we learn that . . .

1. Justification is being declared righteous by God.
2. Adoption is being taken into and made a legal member of another family, as though one were born into that family.
3. Union with Christ is to become one with Him spiritually.

Unknown to them, their plan began to unravel. The beautiful young girl was very impressed with the man and his wife who owned the castle. She had never been around anyone like them before. They were different. They were clean and kind. They talked graciously to one another about interesting things. She began to long to be like them—to live in a civil world where people told the truth and dealt with honor and kindness toward one another.

Something else was happening. The rich man and his wife noticed the young girl. They saw how interested she seemed to be in worthy things. They saw her change from a rather coarse-talking, defensive scullery maid to a kinder, more gracious young lady.

The man and woman had no children, and late one night, as they talked about this beautiful young presence in their home, they developed a plan. They would send her to finishing school, and not only make a lady out of her, but adopt her and make her their daughter.

That very same night, the thieves sneaked into the castle grounds and knocked on the girl's window. "Tomorrow night is the night," hissed the evil leader of the group. "At the stroke of midnight, you open the kitchen door and let us in. We'll take care of things from there!"

The young girl felt terrible. She not only admired the man and woman she worked for, she felt something for them that she had never felt before. She learned later that it was love. She longed to tell them of the plot, but she didn't dare. The thieves would kill her, and if they didn't, she would be imprisoned because of the things she had already stolen herself. She went to bed perhaps the most miserable girl in all the world.

But early the next day, something very unusual happened. The young girl was summoned into the library of the great hall. This was very unusual. No one except the maids ever went into the library. She was terrified. Had they found out about the things she had stolen? Or perhaps the plan of the thieves had been found out, and they would imprison her because of her role in the plot.

Silently she walked down the corridor leading to the library. She glanced about for a chance of escape. Seeing none, she opened the door to the library, slunk in, and stood before the great man and his wife, eyes cast down, awaiting her fate.

Why I Need to Know This

I need to know this so that I can enjoy my Christian experience and relax in my relationship with God. If I understand my security and my union with Christ, it strengthens me to live as I should and creates gratitude and joy.

"We know this will come as a complete surprise to you," they said, "but we would like to adopt you—to make you our own daughter. We would like you to forget your past, and think only of the future with us."

If a gust of wind had forced its way through the slightly opened window, it would have knocked the young girl over. She had come in fearing the unthinkable worst, and now she was hearing the unthinkable best. Be adopted by them? Be rid of her masters? No longer have to lie, cheat, and steal? No longer have to fear imprisonment and death? More than that, she could look forward to a life with meaning, purpose, and fulfillment, to say nothing of that other dim but growing word, love. She might be able to love and be loved. Oh, that would be the greatest of all.

Yet in the very middle of her reverie, she was caught short by the realization that it could not work. She was a thief. She was a liar. She was a sneak. That very night, she was prepared to open the door to the kitchen and let in the thieves who would loot the castle of its treasures. Where could she turn? There was no hope in remaining with the thieves. Nor was there hope in confessing.

With no hope either way, she decided her past would no longer hold her hostage. Better to go to prison with a clear conscience than to live to be a hundred tormented by guilt and remorse. So she confessed the whole thing—the things she had already taken, and the plan to loot the castle that night. Then she waited for the summons to take her to prison.

Instead, the great man before whom she stood astonished her again. "I am not surprised that these thieves have had some hold on you. I have heard how they kidnap innocent infants and turn them into slaves. Yet, the very fact that you told us about everything only confirms our opinion of you. Given a chance, you would choose our life rather than theirs. Our offer still stands. If you will be our daughter, we will have men waiting for the thieves tonight to arrest them. They will be put in prison, and you will never have to worry about them again."

"But what about the things I have already stolen from you? They have been sold, and I cannot get them back," cried the young girl.

After a slight pause, the man said, "We forgive you. Never concern yourself about it again. Your debt is paid because of your love for us. You are no longer guilty."

The great man and woman were true to their word, and the young girl was true to her potential. They adopted her, and she became a lady. And the day came when a handsome young prince met the young lady and fell in love with her. They married. No longer was she simply a lady. She was now a princess. His title was now hers. His fortune was now hers. His power and authority was now hers. His life was now hers. She was one with him, and all that was his became hers.

The moral to the story? We are all the young girl, in bondage to sin and Satan. Yet God offers to adopt us and make us His child. But what about our guilt? Beyond question, we are guilty. Just like the great man in the story, however, God forgives it, through Christ. We marry Christ and become one with Him. All that is His becomes ours. We are children of God, joint heirs with Christ.

What Is Justification?

Justification is being declared righteous by God.

The Evangelical Dictionary of Theology defines justification as "to pronounce, accept, and treat as [righteous], and not . . . liable, and, on the other hand, entitled to all the privileges due to those who have kept the laws." It declares a "verdict of acquittal, and so excluding all possibility of condemnation. Justification thus settles the legal status of the person justified" (593).

Being *declared* righteous by God cannot happen unless we *are* righteous in God's eyes. God does not use sleight-of-hand or smoke and mirrors to get us into heaven. But how can God see us as righteous when we have sin in our lives?

Scripture helps us begin to nail down some answers to this question. Romans 5:1 says, "Therefore, having been justified by faith, we have peace with God through our Lord Jesus Christ." How did we gain this peace with God through justification? Romans 4:2–3 tells us: "For if Abraham was justified by works, he has something to boast about, but not before God. For what does the Scripture say? 'Abraham believed God, and it was accounted to him for righteousness.'"

We see, then, that we are justified the way all people of all times have been justified: through faith. As James Packer states, in his book, *Concise Theology:*

> God's justifying judgment seems strange, for pronouncing sinners righteous may appear to be precisely the unjust action on the judge's part that God's own law forbade (Deuteronomy 25:1; Proverbs 17:15). Yet it is in fact a just judgment, for its basis is the righteousness of Jesus Christ who as "the last Adam" (1 Corinthians 15:45), our representative head acting on our behalf, obeyed the law that bound us and endured the retribution for lawlessness that was our due and so (to use a medieval technical term) "merited" our justification. So we are justified justly, on the basis of justice done (Romans 3:25–26) and Christ's righteousness reckoned to our account (Romans 5:18–19).

When we give our lives to Christ to follow Him, our sins are forgiven, we are born again, and Jesus' righteousness becomes ours. My death could not count for yours because I deserve to die, just as you do. However, Jesus lived perfectly and did not deserve to die. Therefore, in God's eyes, His death could count for ours. Because He was a man, He could die. Because He was God, His death could count for ours. If He were not human, He could not have died, and if He were not God, it wouldn't have mattered if He had.

When we follow Christ His righteousness becomes ours.

Everything Christ made possible (forgiveness of sin and the conferring of righteousness to us) is brought forward, in the mind of God, to the moment of our salvation when we are "crucified in Christ" (Galatians 2:20). We have peace with God (Romans 5:1), we are saved from God's wrath (Romans 5:9), we are glorified (Romans 8:30), and we become heirs, having the hope of eternal life (Titus 3:7).

Milton Carothers, author of the book *Prison to Praise*, had a first-hand experience of what it is like to be declared righteous. During World War II he joined the army. Anxious to get into some serious action and impatient with his slow-moving unit, Carothers went absent without leave but was caught and sentenced to five years in prison. Instead of sending him to prison, though, the judge told him he could serve his term by staying in the army for five years. The judge told him if he left the army before the five years ended, he would have to spend the rest of his sentence in prison. Carothers was released from the army before his five-year term had passed, so he returned to the prosecutor's office to find out where he would be spending the remainder of his sentence. To his surprise and delight, Carothers was told that he had received a pardon from President Truman. The prosecutor explained: "That means your record is completely clear, just as if you had never been involved with the law" (*Illustrations for Biblical Preaching* 209).

What Is Adoption?

Adoption is being taken into and made a legal member of another family, as though one were born into that family.

Much as the beautiful young girl was taken into the family of the wealthy man and woman in the opening story of this chapter, we are taken into God's family. In Ephesians 1:5, the apostle Paul likened this adoption to the Roman concept of adoption, which is discussed in William Barclay's commentary on Ephesians:

When the [Roman] adoption was complete it was complete indeed. The person who had been adopted had all the rights of a legitimate son in his new family and completely lost all rights in his old family. In the eyes of the law he was a new person. So new was he that even all debts and obligations connected with his previous family were abolished as if they had never existed.

That, Paul says, is what God has done for us. We were absolutely in the power of sin and the world. We belonged to the family of Adam, lost and without hope. But God, through Jesus, took us out of that family and adopted us into His; and that adoption wipes out the past and makes us new.

Just as a child has little capacity to grasp how much love it takes for a parent to change its diapers, chauffeur it around, and cope with the demands of adolescence, so we have a limited capacity to grasp how much God loves us. But when we do begin to understand all that He has done for us, the only natural response is galloping gratitude.

Why do parents put up with the tears and tantrums, disobedience and demands of children? One reason is that we love our children and value our relationship with them. We want them to

Adoption places us fully in God's family.

love us and enjoy their relationship with us. It often takes getting some age on the children, and having children themselves, before they begin to appreciate what their parents have done for them. So it is with our relationship with God. He has done so much for us, and wants from us many of the same things earthly parents want from their children, but often we don't begin to grasp it until we gain some maturity.

Even then, we know we are very imperfect children. In spite of that, God chose us before the foundation of the world (Ephesians 1:5) to be His children. Knowing full well, ahead of time, every sin we would ever commit, He adopted us anyway, clearing our name of all the debts of our old family, Adam, through the death of Jesus on the cross.

These things are true whether or not we believe them, and whether or not we "feel" as though they are true. We have learned to accept the fact that the earth is round, even though the landscape before us looks flat. We must do the same regarding our standing before God. We must accept that He loves us, that we are His children, that we are adopted into His family with all the rights and privileges. We may call Him "Abba," which means Papa, or Daddy (Romans 8:15). He has chosen us as His children, to show love and kindness to us forever.

That is what it means to be adopted. It is not merely a legal term. It is a deeply personal term. It is not just that there is an absence of malice, but that there is a presence of love. Envision the best of what earthly families have to offer, and you have the beginning of a glimpse of what heaven has to offer us as God's children.

What Is Union with Christ?

Union with Christ is to become one with Him spiritually.

Again, referring to our opening story, our beautiful young girl grew up to be a lady, and eventually married a handsome young prince. When she did, the Bible says she became one with him (Genesis 2:24). She dropped her last name and took his. She assumed a royal title that would never have come to her any other way than to marry into it. His wealth became hers. His destiny became hers.

Such things happen, not just in fairy tales, but sometimes in real life. Elsewhere in this series, I give the example of Grace Kelly, one of the true megastars in Hollywood in the 50s. She was one of the most beautiful women in the world at the time. She was courted by Prince Rainier of Monaco and eventually married him. Even though she was rich, beautiful, and famous, Grace Kelly was considered a "commoner" by royalty. But this commoner became a princess. After a lavish, storybook wedding, Grace Kelly of Hollywood became Princess Grace of Monaco. Prince Rainier's wealth became hers. His title became hers. His life of royalty became hers as a result of her union with him.

So it is with Christ and us. We become one with Him. We are joined to Him. We become, as the Bible describes it, "in Christ." His wealth, His position, His inheritance, His life become ours. The Bible describes elements of our union with Christ:

We are crucified with Him	Galatians 2:20
We died with Him	Colossians 2:20
We are buried with Him	Romans 6:4
We are made alive with Him	Ephesians 2:5
We are raised with Him	Colossians 3:1
We will suffer with Him	Romans 8:17
We are glorified with Him	Romans 8:17
We are joint heirs with Him	Romans 8:17

This is a judicial union in which God the Father sees us in Christ. When God sees the merit of the cross, He sees Christ and us together. The benefits of Christ's death are credited to us.

But it is more than merely a judicial union with Christ. It is a practical one. Paul wrote in Philippians 4:13, "I can do all things through Christ who strengthens me." In Christ, even our weakness becomes a strength. The apostle Paul was afflicted with a "thorn in the flesh." We don't know exactly what it was, but He asked God three times that it might be taken away from him. Each time, God denied the prayer, but stated that His grace would be sufficient for Paul, and that His power would be perfected in weakness (2 Corinthians 12:9). Paul discovered that his weakness could turn out to be positive: "Most gladly I will rather boast in my infirmities, that the power of Christ may rest upon me. Therefore I take pleasure in infirmities, in reproaches, in needs, in persecutions, in distresses, for Christ's sake. For when I am weak, then I am strong" (9–10).

The fact that we are in Christ and Christ is in us brings us a practical strength for the demands of life that we would not otherwise have. Christians become channels of God's grace and power. When this is properly understood, the Christian need not

Those who are in Christ can draw on His strength.

fear the circumstances of life, need not be distressed when experiencing failure (in the world's eyes, even though it is success in God's), and need not take credit when something good happens. Jesus said, "I am the vine, you are the branches. He who abides in Me, and I in him, bears much fruit; for without Me you can do nothing" (John 15:5). The Christian may always be grateful and happy that God has chosen to use him, but it is bad theology to take credit for results that only God can generate.

Conclusion

Many years ago, my wife and I visited the Grand Canyon with a younger relative of ours. He seemed curiously unmoved by the world's largest hole in the ground, while Margie and I gaped and drooled and mumbled in awe at the sight. Then, after leaving the Grand Canyon, we came upon a smaller canyon, much less impressive. I was ready to stifle a yawn, yet our younger relative was beside himself with awe. "I like this a lot better than the Grand Canyon," he said. "You can see it better." He said the Grand Canyon was so big, to him it looked fake, like a wall mural. This smaller canyon was small enough that his eyes could take it in.

I think that is true about much of God's message in the Bible. His truths are so marvelous, it is hard for us to take them in. Our minds simply are not capable of grasping all the truth. If Publisher's Clearing House knocked on our door and gave us a check for $10 million, we would be delirious with joy. Yet we sometimes miss the joy of God's gracious gift of salvation and our new relationship with Him, perhaps because it is too much for us to take in. But when we stand before Christ in heaven, able at last to grasp the marvelous truths of our union with Him, $10 million will seem insignificant by comparison.

Many remarkable things happen when we are saved. In this chapter, we have looked at only three: we are justified (declared righteous by God based on the work of Christ on the cross that is credited to us); we are adopted (made legal members of God's spiritual family, with all the rights and privileges thereof); and we are united with Christ (joined with Him in His death, His resurrection, and His heavenly life). These are things no amount of money can buy!

Speed Bump

Slow down to be sure you've gotten the main points from this chapter.

Question
Answer

Q1. What is justification?

A1. Justification is being declared *righteous* by God.

Q2. What is adoption?

A2. Adoption is being taken into and made a legal *member* of another family, as though one were born into that family.

Q3. What is union with Christ?

A3. Union with Christ is to become *one* with Him spiritually.

Fill in the Blank

Question
Answer

Q1. What is justification?

A1. Justification is being declared _____ by God.

Q2. What is adoption?

A2. Adoption is being taken into and made a legal _____ of another family, as though one were born into that family.

Q3. What is union with Christ?

A3. Union with Christ is to become ___ with Him spiritually.

For Further Thought and Discussion

1. What would you say, in your own words, is the basis for being declared righteous by God? Do you feel righteous before God? If/when you don't, how would you verify it from Scripture?

2. Imagine that you have been adopted by a rich, powerful, and famous family. You become their only child, heir to their fortune and position. What insights from that hypothetical situation can you apply to your adoption by God?

3. What, to you, is the single most significant consequence of being united with Christ? Why?

What If I Don't Believe?

If I don't understand and/or believe what happens when I am saved, it can cause me to fall short of the joyful experience God wants me to have. This not only diminishes my life on earth, but also makes me a less effective witness of the message of salvation.

For Further Study

1. Scripture

- Romans 4:3
- Romans 5:1
- Romans 8:1, 14–17
- Ephesians 1:5
- Ephesians 2:5

2. Books

How to Be Born Again, Billy Graham
Salvation: God's Amazing Plan, Millard Erickson

In God's faithfulness lies eternal security.
■ Corrie ten Boom (1892–1983)

Am I Secure in God's Love?

Fear is a terrible thing. I can remember several times in my life when I was truly terrified. One time as a teenager I decided, for reasons that no longer seem sufficient, to climb to the top of a city water tower. There was a catwalk that encircled the water tank about halfway up, and I thought it would be interesting to go up there and look around.

In this chapter we learn that . . .

1. Assurance is the confidence that Christians are, in fact, saved.
2. Eternal security is the belief that genuine Christians will always be saved.

As I began climbing the rickety ladder, getting perhaps fifty feet off the ground, I was suddenly seized with panic. I looked down (they say you are never supposed to look down, and in retrospect, it seems like good advice), and every muscle in my body turned to mush. I began losing my grip. My mouth went dry. I could not keep my mind from envisioning the rung I was holding onto pulling loose from the ladder, sending me plunging upside down to the earth below. I wrapped my arms and legs through the rungs of the ladder so that I could keep from falling, even though my muscles had abandoned me.

I stayed there for I don't know how long, unable to go up or down. I finally worked out a system by which I entangled my limbs so thoroughly in the rungs and side of the ladder that I would not have fallen off if I had passed out. Then, using modified versions of that position, I squirmed my way back down to the ground. Safe! What a wonderful feeling it was to be safe!

Another time I remember being in a rather violent storm in an airplane. The turbulence had people singing choruses to calm their fear. The plane dropped noticeably for a second. All together, as though directed by an invisible conductor, everyone said, "Ooooooooooo!"

A little while later, it dropped for a couple of seconds. On cue, everyone sang, "Ooooohhhhh!"

Sometime later, the plane dropped for several seconds, then abruptly surged upward again, creaking and groaning. In perfect unison, everyone cried, "YAAAAAHHHH!"

On the outside, I was calm as the Sphinx. On the inside, I was leading the choir. I was screaming, "Oh God, if you get me off this airplane alive, I promise I'll never get on another airplane as long as I live!"

Finally, after being tossed around pretty badly for a long time, we lurched and bobbed onto the runway. Safe! What a wonderful feeling it was to be safe.

Why I Need to Know This

I need to know this so that I can have confidence, joy, and peace in my Christian life. The assurance that we are secure in God's love is fundamental to the abundant life He wants to give us.

Being safe is the kind of thing we take for granted until we lose it. And when we lose it, when we are in an unsafe situation, we realize how precious safety is.

As unnerving as these experiences were, none of them compare to having to live in prolonged fear. Christians in some other countries worship in constant fear that someone will kick the door in and find them. People who live in war zones where bombing is being carried on live with ongoing fear. I remember as a child going to bed each night afraid that the United States and the (then) Soviet Union would go to nuclear war with each other and blow up the planet. It was like a pain that never went away.

But the worst fear I have ever lived with is the fear that I might die and go to hell. I remember vividly two instances that occurred *before* I became a Christian. One Sunday evening when I was a junior in high school, I was home alone reading the newspaper. Someone had written an article observing that, comparing modern events with biblical prophecy, the end of the world might be imminent. Even though I was not a Christian, I believed the Bible and was seized with runaway terror. I drove to the parsonage of a local pastor and knocked on the door. He was reading the newspaper, too. I showed him the article and asked him what he thought of it. He merely said there might be something to it. Then he prayed for me, and I went home. I couldn't believe the minister didn't have any more wisdom or comfort than that. I was still terrified and hoped that somehow I could find God before the end of the world came.

Another instance happened when I was a freshman in college. I was playing drums in a rock band, and the rhythm guitarist and I were coming back from an engagement. He was driving and was drunk as a skunk. It began raining so hard that we couldn't see ten car lengths ahead of us, and he was hurtling us down the road in that death-capsule at more than seventy miles an hour. I begged, threatened, and pleaded for him to slow down so he didn't rear-end someone, but in his highly inebriated state, my supplications fell on deaf ears. So I got into the back seat and lay down on the floor. I figured if we had an accident, that would be the safest place to be.

Simply through luck (from a human perspective), nothing happened to us that day, but I remember thinking, *I need to become a Christian sooner or later, and it had better be sooner, because there might not be any "later."* At that point I didn't know how, so I just continued on in my fear of dying, hoping that somehow I could come to meet God before it was too late. In the providence of God, I became a Christian just a few months after that.

The final instance came after I had been a Christian for a number of years. I began thinking that, when I had become a Christian, it had been in a time of personal crisis, and, like a man drowning at sea, I had grabbed for the closest thing that I thought might keep me afloat, which was Christianity. But after a while I began to question if I had made the right decision. What if it wasn't true? What if something else were true? I hadn't really investigated Christianity or other alternatives at all. So what if I were wrong?

With that, I entered another period in which I lived in dread of dying. I feared flying, I feared going to sleep at night, I feared riding in a car with anyone I did not think was a good driver. It was like living with chronic pain. I became convinced that there are few things worse than the constant fear that you might die and go to hell.

The purpose of this chapter is to investigate what the Bible says about our security as a believer. Can we be safe? Can we feel safe? Can we be free of that dreadful weight called fear hung around our necks?

We can.

What Is Assurance?

Assurance is the confidence that Christians are, in fact, saved.

It is not uncommon for Christians to struggle with doubts as to whether or not they are saved. This can stem from several things. First, it may grow out of a misunderstanding of what happens when one becomes a Christian. For example, when I committed my life to Christ as a college student, I thought I ought to feel something. Someone told me that the Holy Spirit **Assurance is more** would come into my heart, take up residence **than feelings.** within me, and give me the power to begin to live the life God wanted me to live. It seemed reasonable to me that I would feel something, and when I didn't, I was doubtful about whether anything had actually happened when I gave my life to Christ. The person I was talking with at the time assured me that the Bible did not say that we would feel anything, but that if I truly believed in and committed my life to Christ, I was born again, saved, and that I should take the testimony of Scripture by faith, rather than looking for some subjective emotional experience. I wasn't totally convinced, but took his word for it for the time being.

Later, several friends who knew the Scriptures well talked me through the salvation passages and finally persuaded me that I was, as I would have put it, probably a Christian, but I struggled with occasional doubts for years after that.

After I had been a Christian for more than ten years, I was suddenly and unexpectedly afflicted with raging doubt about my salvation. As I look back on it, I think it was a ploy by the devil to derail me in my Christian life. However, God turned it around and used it to give me greater-than-ever confidence in my salvation.

I couldn't shake the insecurity that had lingered since my salvation experience. I became deeply troubled much of the time. I lost sight of the promises of God, and peace fled from me like rats from a sinking ship. But in the midst of the worst doubts, I grabbed hold of the Scripture like a life raft and had my assurance restored. The passages that linked together to buoy me up were:

1. Psalm 130:4, "There is forgiveness with You, that You may be feared." This passage told me that it was possible to be forgiven.

2. John 6:37, "The one who comes to Me I will by no means cast out." I had believed in Jesus. I had asked Him to save me. So, this passage assured me that, since I had come to Jesus, He would not cast me out.

3. 1 John 5:12, "He who has the Son has life; he who does not have the Son of God does not have life." I had come to Jesus. He had not cast me out. Therefore, I had life. I was forgiven. I was saved. What a relief!

Other times when people struggle with doubts about their salvation it might be because of the imperfection of their lifestyle. Their doubts can come from at least two directions. People who tend toward perfectionism struggle with the inability to eradicate all sin—not only not doing the things they're not supposed to, but also doing all the things they should do. This is a tremendous burden, because we can get compulsive about perfection and never measure up to our own expectations, or the expectations we think God has of us. Doubts also can come from falling back into obvious sin. There is no perfectionism at work here; these people are sinning blatantly. They know it, and usually others know it. Both of these scenarios can cause doubts about salvation, and God deals with each differently.

Sin in one's life can cause doubts about salvation.

There are still other sources of doubt concerning a person's salvation. For example, if one grew up in another religion and converted to Christianity, the people he grew up with might accuse him of having left the only "true" faith.

How can we deal with our doubts? How can we know that God has saved us? I believe there are three related ways we can know we are saved and enjoy the blessing of assurance.

Scripture—God's Word on It

To deal with our doubt about salvation, we must first look at the ways the Bible tells us we can have assurance of our salvation. The Bible tells us that "as many as received [Jesus], to them He gave the right to become children of God, to those who believe in His name" (John 1:12). So true faith in Christ results in our being a child of God.

In Romans 10:13, we read, "Whoever calls upon the name of the Lord shall be saved." The real question, then, is simple: "Do you believe in, and have you received Jesus as your savior—

have you trusted in Christ as your only savior and given your life to Him?" If the answer is "yes," then God says "You are a child of Mine."

This is true regardless of how we feel. Our feelings can be deceiving. "For if our hearts condemn us, God is greater than our heart, and knows all things" (1 John 3:20).

God does not want us to be anxious about our relationship to Him, once it has been established. As John summarized near the end of his first letter, "These things I have written to you who believe in the name of the Son of God, that you may *know* that you have eternal life, and that you may *continue to believe* in the name of the Son of God" (1 John 5:13, italics added).

Change—the Dynamics of Daily Experience

Assurance of salvation also can come from a changed life. Genuinely new life manifests itself in new attitudes, new values, and new behavior. Some who claim to have become a Christian manifest no change whatsoever in their behavior. In his book, *Loving God*, Chuck Colson tells the story of Mickey Cohen, a Los Angeles gangster in the late '40s who supposedly became a Christian through Billy Graham's early ministry. But he didn't change his behavior or his mob connections. When challenged about it, he said, "You never told me that I had to give up my career. You never told me that I had to give up my friends. There are Christian movie stars, Christian athletes, Christian businessmen. So what's the matter with being a Christian gangster? If I have to give up all that—if that's Christianity—count me out" (92).

His lack of outward change was a tip-off that no change had taken place on the inside. As the apostle John wrote, "They went out from us, but they were not of us; for if they had been of us, they would have continued with us; but they went out that they might be made manifest, that none of them were of us" (1 John 2:19). He is saying that when someone turns his back on Christianity, it is probably a sign that he never was a true Christian.

The apostle Peter says, in 2 Peter 1:5–10, that if we want to be sure of our salvation we must look at our lifestyle. There will be godly growth. True, we may struggle with not seeing the degree of change we would like, but we will see some change. In fact, the very existence of such a struggle suggests that the person who claims faith in Christ is truly saved.

Scripture passages that suggest the need for change are numerous. First Peter 2:2 says, "As newborn babes, desire the pure milk of the word, that you may grow thereby." Romans 12:2 says, "Do not be conformed to this world, but be transformed by the renewing of your mind." Many other passages trumpet the same theme. Change is a vital sign of spiritual life.

Change is a vital sign of spiritual life.

Christians can sin, and perfectionists who doubt their salvation because of sin must recognize this (1 John 1:8) and rest in God's faithfulness when they confess this sin (1 John 1:9). John also reminds us that when we sin "We have an Advocate with the Father, Jesus Christ the righteous" (1 John 2:1). Only those whose pattern of living includes ongoing, willful, unrepentant sin does the Bible give reason to doubt their salvation.

Personal change was what finally convinced me of my own salvation. I began to see changes in my life that I had tried to achieve before I became a Christian, and now they were happening, seemingly because of forces in my life greater than I. When I compared that to verses in the Bible that said the Holy Spirit would bring about change in my life, I became convinced that I was, indeed, a Christian.

Faithfulness—Pleasing God and Caring about Others

Another evidence of salvation is increased faithfulness in obeying the commands of Scripture. "Whoever keeps His word, truly the love of God is perfected in him. By this we know that we are in Him" (1 John 2:5). And again, "He who keeps His commandments abides in Him, and He in him" (1 John 3:24).

The apostle John also mentioned a love for the brethren as an indication of salvation: "We know that we have passed from death to life, because we love the brethren" (1 John 3:14). I don't think this means that we love perfectly every single hard-to-love Christian in our life. Rather, I think it means that, generally, we love other Christians—that we enjoy their company, make friends among them, want to help them, and care about their welfare. It means, I think, that we identify with them and consider ourselves one of them.

Faithfulness and fellowship are indications of salvation.

Thus we have more to go on than our "feelings" to determine whether or not we are saved. We receive assurance from

God's word, from our daily walk of faith, and from our new attitude toward God and others.

We really should be as confident of our relationship to Christ as we are of our relationship to our natural family or our spouse. We don't normally question whose children we are; we are part of a particular family unit. When God says we are now members of His family, we need to rest in that. Likewise, we never have to stop and think about our marital status—either we are married or we are not. In Ephesians 5 Paul compares our relationship to Christ to that between a husband and wife, loving and supporting each other forever.

What Is Eternal Security?

Eternal security is the belief that genuine Christians will always be saved.

One of the standard questions for theological debate over the last two thousand years has been whether or not a Christian could lose his salvation. Some passages seem to suggest one can lose his salvation, and others seem to suggest that one cannot. It is a delicate matter to reconcile these passages, and as a result, Protestant Christianity has historically been divided between the two views represented by John Calvin and Jacobus Arminius.

Calvinism: One group, including those called "Calvinists," after John Calvin, a leader of the Protestant reformation in the 1500s, believe that a person who is genuinely saved cannot lose his salvation. He may "backslide" for a time into sinful behavior, but he will never be lost, since our salvation came through the grace of God in the first place. This position often is stated as "once saved, always saved."

The passages that support this understanding of Scripture include John 10:27–30:

> My sheep hear My voice, and I know them, and they follow Me. And I give them eternal life, and they shall never perish; neither shall anyone snatch them out of My hand. My Father, who has given them to Me, is greater than all; and no one is able to snatch them out of My Father's hand. I and My Father are one.

This seems to be a clear statement that once a person has been given to Christ by God, he is eternally secure. This understanding is bolstered by Romans 8:35–39:

Who shall separate us from the love of Christ? Shall tribulation, or distress, or persecution, or famine, or nakedness, or peril, or sword? As it is written: *For Your sake we are killed all day long; We are accounted as sheep for the slaughter.* Yet in all these things we are more than conquerors through Him who loved us. For I am persuaded that neither death nor life, nor angels nor principalities nor powers, nor things present nor things to come, nor height nor depth, nor any other created thing, shall be able to separate us from the love of God which is in Christ Jesus.

Other passages that reinforce this perspective are Philippians 1:6, Romans 8:29, Romans 11:29, 2 Timothy 1:12, Ephesians 1:13–14, and 1 Peter 1:5.

In addition to these Scripture passages, there is also the logical (theological) argument that goes along with them. When a person is born again, he is spiritually reborn through a work of the Holy Spirit. Ephesians 2:8 states that this salvation is not a work of ourselves, but is a gift of God. We are given a new spirit that is created "according to God, in true righteousness and holiness" (Ephesians 4:24).

Our righteousness and holiness are not yet perfected, however. Even reborn believers still must fight against a residue of sin remaining in them. Romans 7:19–20 says that "the good that I will to do, I do not do; but the evil I will not to do, that I practice. Now if I do what I will not to do, it is no longer I who do it, but sin that dwells in me." Nevertheless, this sin in the true believer never can cancel the gift of life and peace with God given freely because of Jesus. Based on this truth, the apostle Paul triumphantly declares, "There is therefore now no condemnation to those who are in Christ Jesus" (8:1).

How, then, could one lose his salvation, since that would require regeneration in reverse—degeneration into death again, slipping from a position that we did not attain ourselves anyway, but which God gave us? "For if when we were enemies we were reconciled to God through the death of His Son, much more, having been reconciled, we shall be saved by His life" (Romans 5:10). This simply reinforces Romans 8:29, "For whom He foreknew, He also predestined to be conformed to the image of His Son, that He might be the firstborn among many brethren."

One of the strongest arguments for people being able to lose their salvation seems to me to be people who gave every evidence of having been Christians but then turned their backs on it.

So how can we explain that? They seemed to be genuine Christians who turned away from the faith, and then for years lived the kind of a lifestyle described in Galatians 5:19–21 of people who cannot inherit the kingdom of God.

Calvinists point to the book of 1 Corinthians, which suggests that Christians can fall into dreadful sin and still be Christians. However, Hebrews 12:5–11 teaches that Christians who do fall into sin will be chastened for their sin. The passages together, to the Calvinist position, seem to suggest that Christians who sin flagrantly for extended periods of time will experience such chastening from the Lord that they might become weak, or sick, or even die (1 Corinthians 11:30)! That is, God may take the life of a flagrantly sinning Christian. This chastening occurs so that "we may not be condemned with the world" (11:32). It seems that God is committed to seeing us through to heaven once we are children of His, but that we are not free to live like the devil unless we want to experience the "severe mercy" of God.

So what about those who seem to be genuine Christians and then turn away from the faith but don't become weak, sick, or die from the chastening hand of God? Those who hold to eternal security might say we cannot know their hearts. We must leave their destiny with God. However, because of Hebrews 12:5–11, the fact that they seem not to be chastened by God may indicate that they only seemed to be saved, but actually were not, as those in 1 John 2:19, and the challenge of 2 Corinthians 13:5, "to examine themselves to see if they are in the faith," may be in order.

Having qualified that, however, Paul said of the Philippian believers that he was "confident of this very thing, that He who has begun a good work in you will complete it until the day of Jesus Christ" (1:6). Of himself, he said, "I know whom I have believed and am persuaded that He is able to keep what I have committed to Him until that Day" (2 Timothy 1:12). The Calvinist position points to Ephesians, where we see, concerning our salvation, that it is the result of:

- His will, not ours (1:5)
- His grace, not ours (1:6–7)
- His purpose, not ours (1:11)
- His power, not ours (1:12, 14)
- His calling, not ours (1:18).

According to these passages, it seems that we did not save ourselves. He saved us. We do not keep ourselves. He keeps us. We are not secure in ourselves. We are secure in Him.

Arminianism: Another group, including those called Arminians, after the 16th century Dutch theologian, Jacobus Arminius, believe that it is possible to lose one's salvation. Most of these contend that those who lose their salvation can regain it, although some in the past contended that they cannot. The Scripture passages usually used to support this understanding include Hebrews 6:4–6:

> For it is impossible for those who were once enlightened, and have tasted the heavenly gift, and have become partakers of the Holy Spirit, and have tasted the good word of God and the powers of the age to come, if they fall away, to renew them again to repentance, since they crucify again for themselves the Son of God, and put Him to an open shame.

Further evidence for this position is often cited in the writings of the apostle Paul. In 1 Corinthians 9:27, we read, "But I discipline my body and bring it into subjection, lest, when I have preached to others, I myself should become disqualified." In this same emphasis, he wrote to the Galatians, "You have become estranged from Christ, you who attempt to be justified by law; for you have fallen from grace" (5:4). Other passages often cited include Mark 13:13, 1 Corinthians 15:2, and Hebrews 10:28–29.

In addition to these passages is added the logical (theological) argument that if, by an act of our own free will we accept Christ, cannot we, by an act of our own free will, knowingly reject Him? God graciously provided the means to salvation, but each individual must choose whether or not to accept—or keep—His grace gift. Also, consider Galatians 5:19–21:

> Now the works of the flesh are evident, which are: adultery, fornication, uncleanness, lewdness, idolatry, sorcery, hatred, contentions, jealousies, outbursts of wrath, selfish ambitions, dissensions, heresies, envy, murders, drunkenness, revelries, and the like; of which I tell you beforehand, just as I also told you in time past, that those who practice such things will not inherit the kingdom of God.

Add to this passage the fact that many people have claimed, and seemingly demonstrated to be Christians, and then have fallen back into these practices. In such cases, the text seems clearly to say they will not inherit the kingdom of God. The fact that external forces cannot "snatch them out of My Father's hand" as cited earlier (John 10:29) still leaves open the possibility of personal rebellion and rejection of saving grace.

These, then, are the two major positions regarding eternal security, though there are a number of variations of each view.

Arminians insist that "whosoever" may come to Christ—or reject Him. While I believe the Calvinistic view, there are godly, well-educated, and intelligent people on both sides of this issue, and the positions are held strongly, since one's perspective on the issue can so directly affect one's daily spiritual life. It seems to be one of those issues on which the Bible says we must become persuaded in our own mind (Romans 14:5). For a further discussion of the issues concerning eternal security, look into the books at the end of this chapter.

Conclusion

While earnest Christians disagree about whether or not genuine believers may willfully renounce Christ and lose the gift of salvation, one thing is certain: God will save whoever comes to Him in faith. He will not turn anyone away. We can know that we are saved by heeding the teaching of Scripture regarding how we are saved, and by checking our lives against the things that the Bible says will be true of genuine believers. And, if we follow Him, we can rest in the assurance that God will keep us safe until we go to be with Him.

Speed Bump

Slow down to be sure you've gotten the main points from this chapter.

Question **A**nswer

Q1. What is assurance?

A1. Assurance is the *confidence* that Christians are, in fact, saved.

Q2. What is eternal security?

A2. Eternal security is the belief that genuine Christians will *always* be saved.

Fill in the Blank

Question   **Q1.** What is assurance?

Answer   **A1.** Assurance is the _____ that Christians are, in fact, saved.

Q2. What is eternal security?

A2. Eternal security is the belief that genuine Christians will _____ be saved.

For Further Thought and Discussion

1. Have you ever struggled with doubts about your salvation? What Scripture passages have been most helpful in giving you assurance?

2. Have you ever struggled with fears that you might lose your salvation? Why do you think you have/had those fears? Do the Scriptures in this chapter persuade you of your eternal security? Why or why not?

What If I Don't Believe?

If I don't believe I am secure in God's love, I am likely to be tormented by doubts and fear, robbing me of my peace and joy in the Christian life. It may also enslave me to a life of legalism, trying to keep my good works in sufficient supply so that I will not lose my salvation.

For Further Study

1. Scripture

- Psalm 130:4
- John 6:37
- John 10:27–30
- Romans 8:35–39
- Ephesians 1:1–18
- Hebrews 6:4–6
- 1 Peter 2:2

- 1 John 2:5
- 1 John 5:12

2. Books

How to Be Born Again, Billy Graham
Eternal Security, Charles Stanley
A Theology of Love, Mildred Wynkoop

What would my church be like if every
member were just like me?
■ Anonymous

8

What Difference Should My Salvation Make to the Church?

It doesn't take much to go wrong with the body before we notice it. A hangnail starts us whimpering. A headache gets us groaning. A slipped disk has us begging for mercy. You can drop a cockroach six feet to a hard floor, and it will get up, shake itself off, and go on its way unaffected. But humans can't even fall to their knees without risk of serious injury. Our bodies are fragile, sensitive things.

I have read that cells in the body replace themselves with such frequency that we get a brand-new body every seven years. If that's the case, the first three bodies I had were each an improvement on the previous ones. On my fourth body, I broke even. On all subsequent bodies, I have been going downhill.

My third body could high jump almost seven feet. With floor mats and friends to "spot" me so I wouldn't break my neck, I once jumped high enough to kick a basketball rim (ten feet). I could run for miles. I could lift weights until I was completely fatigued and get up stronger the next morning. I could throw a round ball from twenty feet away through a slightly larger orange hoop ten feet off the ground with nearly 50 percent accuracy. I could see the eyelash of a gnat on the end of my nose, and read an interstate road sign a mile away. Oh, how I long for that third body. Everything worked—even better than worked. It moved with strength, endurance, and skill.

As the decades have passed since that third body, the decline has been alarming. I now have to think twice about jumping over a crack in the sidewalk. I can't run any distance without my back and feet aching and my lungs threatening to spontaneously combust. When I lift weights, I pull muscles rather than get stronger. I can't even *throw* a basketball twenty feet, let alone put it through the hoop. I can still read the interstate road signs a mile away (perhaps the last vestige of my third body), but I now need reading glasses to find my fork and spoon. I have become acutely aware of how the whole body is limited when one or more of its parts doesn't do its job. How I long for heaven and a body that works as it should.

In this chapter I learn that . . .

1. I join the body by becoming a Christian.
2. My gift to the body is to use my spiritual gift in its behalf.
3. My duty is to commit myself to the body's welfare.

The Bible compares the church to a body. The church is the totality of all believers in Jesus, and we are supposed to work together in harmony like my third body did. We are supposed to be faster than a speeding bullet, more powerful than a locomotive, and able to leap tall buildings with a single bound. When we don't work together in harmony, we become like my seventh body—uncooperative, uncoordinated, and unconditioned. We limp and gimp and shuffle through life instead of leaping and lifting and running.

I don't have a choice as to which body I live in. That's determined by my genetics and life experiences. But we can influence what kind of body the church is. It can be an invalid or an Olympic athlete, depending on our level of trust and obedience to the Lord.

Of course, we cannot determine how others fulfill their role in the body, but we can determine how we fulfill ours. When we get saved, it will make a difference how we relate to the church. So if it is up to us, let the body leap and lift and run. Each of us, when we become a Christian, has a God-given role to play in the church, and we should play it well!

How Do I Join the Body?

I join the body by becoming a Christian.

Salvation is the door into the church. Step through the door of salvation, and you are automatically in the church—not a local church, of course, but the universal church, the totality of all believers in Jesus. One can be in a local church and not be in the universal church, and while it is not desirable, one can be in the universal church without being in a local church.

As soon as we step through the door of salvation, we become "one" with all the other members of the body. Their welfare depends on us, and our welfare depends on them. We don't often realize this. We often go through life with struggles that we assume we must bear alone, not realizing that in a more perfect world the other members of the body would be there to help us through them.

Why I Need to Know This

I need to know this so that I will make an adequate commitment to the welfare of the body of Christ. It is easy to think that someone else will make sure the church needs what it gets. But it is up to each of us. If we are not contributing what we can to the body, then we are partially responsible for its weaknesses and shortcomings.

Coming to salvation is a very individual thing. Every person stands before God alone. Even though others may help us, it is our sin that must be forgiven, it is our will that must be redirected, it is our life that must be given to Christ. The fact that we live in a "Christian" nation does not make us a Christian. The fact that our parents are Christians does not make us a Christian. The fact that we may be members of a local church does not make us a Christian. The only thing that makes us a Christian is to believe in and receive Christ as our God and savior (John 1:12, Titus 3:4–5). That very individual decision which we must make alone, in the solitude of our soul, is the last decision we make without regard for our fellow members of the body of Christ. After that, we must realize that we are part of a whole that we need, and which needs us.

What Is My Gift to the Body?

My gift to the body is to use my spiritual gift in its behalf.

First Peter 4:10 says, "As each one has received a gift, minister it to one another, as good stewards of the manifold grace of God." From this we learn three things: (1) Each of us has a gift; (2) its use is not optional; we are obligated to use it; and (3) we are to use it to benefit one another in the body of Christ.

People understand spiritual gifts in various ways. Generally speaking, a spiritual gift is a God-given ability to minister to others. I find it helpful, for the purpose of this chapter, to recognize three different kinds of spiritual gifts.

Office Gifts. This kind of gift is given to the church at large through gifted individuals (Ephesians 4:11). Office gifts support the functions of the apostle, prophet, evangelist, and pastor-teacher. While there is not widespread common understanding of these gifts, I understand the office gifts of apostle and prophet, which were used to establish the church (Ephesians 2:20), to have disappeared, and the gifts of evangelist and pastor-teacher, which are used to propagate the church, to be still in force. There are some folk, however, who believe all four still exist, and there are a few who believe that none of them still exist.

Special Gifts. A second category of gift I find helpful to classify as "special gifts." A representative list is found in 1 Corinthians 12:4–10. People have significant differences in their understanding of these gifts. Many believe they are still in force today, while others believe they have disappeared, and still others believe that a reduced form of them exists today, but they are not given as fully as they once were.

Service Gifts. Concerning a third list of gifts, however, there is almost full agreement. Almost everyone agrees these gifts are in full force today. These are the gifts I want to discuss, because they fit the purpose of this chapter. The service gifts are found in Romans 12:6–8:

1. *Prophecy.* Some debate surrounds the meaning of this term. Some understand prophecy as being able to foretell the future. While I believe that is one of the special gifts, this list of gifts in all other instances seems to be service gifts, and it seems out of context to understand this as one special gift in a list of six service gifts. Within the context of this passage, I think it is reasonable to understand prophecy in light of the description in 1 Corinthians 14:3 which says, "He who prophesies speaks edification and exhortation and comfort to men." With this understanding, we would understand prophecy in this passage as the gift of being divinely skilled at speaking edification, exhortation, and comfort to people.

2. *Ministry.* This word is translated "service" in the NASB and NIV translations. It means to serve and help meet the practical needs of others. This word is used in Luke 10:40 when Jesus went to the home of two sisters, Mary and Martha. Mary sat at Jesus' feet and listened to him, but "Martha was distracted with

much serving, and she approached Him and said, 'Lord, do You not care that my sister has left me to serve alone? Therefore tell her to help me.'" Within the broader context, the word means "ministry" in the sense of serving others. Some people are divinely gifted with this inclination and skill.

3. *Teaching.* This word means to instruct others so that they understand the truth of Scripture and spiritual truth. We read this word in 2 Timothy 2:2, "And the things that you have heard from me among many witnesses, commit these to faithful men who will be able to teach others also." We are all to teach others in varying capacities, but some people are divinely gifted to be able to help others understand the truth of Scripture.

4. *Exhortation.* This word means, literally, to call toward to help. Therefore it sometimes is translated comfort. It also can carry the idea of admonishing or encouraging toward virtue. It is used related to those whom you do not have the authority to command, but from whom you strongly desire compliance. After a strongly written letter, the writer of Hebrews says, "I appeal to you, brethren, bear with the word of exhortation" (Hebrews 13:22). Some Christians are divinely gifted to see what needs to be done and to strongly urge others to do it.

5. *Giving.* This word is used in Luke 3:11 where John the Baptist is instructing his followers in Christian graces. He says that if you have two tunics, give one to the person who has none; and he who has food, let him do likewise. It is used also in Ephesians 4:28 where the apostle Paul wrote, "Let him who stole steal no longer, but rather let him labor, working with his hands what is good, that he may have something to give to him who has need." These verses help us capture the essence of what it means to give to others. It means that out of your abundance, you share with those in need. Some people are divinely gifted to see, care about, and respond to those in need by sharing with them.

6. *Leading.* This is the gift of leading others. In 1 Thessalonians 5:12–13, we read, "Now we ask you, brothers, to respect those who work hard among you, who are over you in the Lord and who admonish you. Hold them in the highest regard in love because of their work" (NIV). The words "over you" are translated from the same word as "leading." This word is found in 1 Timothy 3:4, where we read that an elder is one who "rules

his own house well" or "manages his own house well" (NASB). Of course, those who lead are to do so with the spirit and heart of a shepherd, not lording it over them, but being an example of Christ (1 Peter 5:2–4). Some people are divinely gifted to be able to do this.

7. *Mercy.* This gift is the special regard to the misery of others, especially when the misery is a consequence of sin. We read this capacity of God in Ephesians 2:4–5, "But God, who is rich in mercy, because of His great love with which He loved us, even when we were dead in trespasses, made us alive together with Christ." This quality of God's mercy is also found in individuals, and in some to a high degree.

We all have one or more of these service gifts, to lesser or greater degrees. Whatever our gift, we are to employ it in serving one another.

What Is My Christian Duty to the Body?

My duty is to commit myself to the body's welfare.

In fact, every individual's spiritual gift is also a common responsibility for everyone else (1 Peter 4:10; Galatians 6:10). We may have one or more of the "service gifts" listed in Romans 12, but probably no one has them all. Yet all of us are responsible to do all the things in the list of service gifts. The following chart shows the relationship between the gift in Romans 12 and a corresponding command elsewhere in the Bible that is applicable to every Christian, even if we don't have the gift.

In light of these service gifts, there are certain things that we are gifted to do, and there are certain things we are responsible to do, whether or not we feel gifted to do them. For example, some people are gifted to evangelize others. They do it naturally and skillfully, while others feel awkward and ill-equipped. Nevertheless, we are all responsible to evangelize others—to share our faith and experience with Christ with others. Matthew 28:19–20 is a commission to all Christians to take the message of salvation by grace through faith in Christ to the ends of the world. In addition, 2 Timothy 4:5 tells us to "do the work of an evangelist."

In addition to ministering our spiritual gift (as well as being responsible in all of the "gift" areas), the Bible is full of state-

Romans 12 gift	Common command
prophecy (speaking, edification)	Therefore let us pursue . . . the things by which one may edify another (Romans 14:19). Comfort each other and edify one another (1 Thessalonians 5:11).
ministering (helping others in need)	You must support the weak (Acts 20:35). Comfort the fainthearted, uphold the weak (1 Thessalonians 5:14).
teaching (helping others understand spiritual truth)	[Commit truth] to faithful men who will be able to teach others also (2 Timothy 2:2).
exhortation (encouraging and challenging others)	Encourage one another daily (Hebrews 3:13, NIV). If your brother sins against you, rebuke him (Luke 17:3).
giving (meeting others' financial needs)	Let each one give as he purposes in his heart (2 Corinthians 9:7).
leading (helping others achieve a goal)	Manage [lead your] own family well (1 Timothy 3:4).
mercy (showing love and compassion to others)	Blessed are the merciful for they shall obtain mercy (Matthew 5:7).

ments about things we are to do for one another. Some of the more powerful admonitions are found in Romans:

Romans 12:10   Be devoted to one another in brotherly love.
Romans 12:10   Give preference to one another in honor.
Romans 12:16   Be of the same mind toward one another.
Romans 13:8   Love one another.
Romans 14:19   Make for peace and the building up of one another.
Romans 15:5   Be of the same mind with one another.
Romans 15:7   Accept one another.
Romans 15:14   Admonish one another.
Romans 16:16   Greet one another.

The point of these verses is that we are to live in love and unity with other Christians. In John 13:34–35, Jesus said, "A new commandment I give to you, that you love one another; as I have loved you, that you also love one another. By this all will know that you are My disciples, if you have love for one another." This powerful and profound verse tells us that the mark or badge of Christians is supposed to be their love for one another. Just as the physical body is to function in unity and harmony with itself—and if it doesn't it is considered dysfunctional—so the spiritual body of Christ is supposed to function in unity and harmony with itself.

This truth is further advanced in Ephesians 4:3, where we read, "[Endeavor] to keep the unity of the Spirit in the bond of peace." From this and other verses, we learn that, as Christians, we do have unity in Christ. The Scripture says, "There is one

Our challenge is to give practical expression to our spiritual unity.

body and one Spirit, just as you were called in one hope of your calling; one Lord, one faith, one baptism; one God and Father of all, who is above all, and through all, and in you all" (Ephesians 4:4–6). In Ephesians 2:21–22, we read, "The whole building, being fitted together, grows into a holy temple in the Lord, in whom you also are being built together for a dwelling place of God in the spirit." And finally, in Galatians 3:28, we read, "There is neither Jew nor Greek, there is neither slave nor free, there is neither male nor female; for you are all one in Christ Jesus."

From these passages, we see that spiritual unity does exist among Christians. We *are* spiritually united in Christ. But our task is to live out, on a physical level, the unity that already exists on a spiritual level.

This, of course, is easier said than done. Frankly, not all Christians are easy to live with. Someone has said, with tongue only slightly in cheek, to live above with saints we love, oh, that will be glory. To live below with saints we know, well, that's another story. And so it is. People who are difficult to be around as non-Christians are also often difficult to live around as Christians. Simply becoming a Christian does not automatically make it easy to win friends and influence people. And, certainly, both parties have to be committed to the same goal. You might try to live in unity with someone else who wants little to do with you. I have witnessed marriages that have broken up when one partner wanted out and the other desperately wanted to stay together. We cannot live in unity with others who refuse to live in unity. But to the degree that it depends on us, we are to live in unity with others.

This does not mean we will be best friends with all Christians. It just means that we are to be obedient to the Scriptures, and love one another as Christ has loved us. This does not mean that we are emotionally bonded to each of them, but that we direct our will toward the good of others, and as we are able to do good for other Christians, we do. And we give up selfish ambition for the sake of unity with others (Philippians 2:1–4).

Conclusion

Life in Christ through the church is not an option. Spiritual life apart from the church is abnormal and in violation of the mission of Jesus to create a new community of believers. His body, by definition, is a whole made up of many members interconnected with one another. A simple but accurate analogy is that of a newborn human life; it is inconceivable that newborns would live on their own. The choice of some adults to be virtual spiritual hermits is not only a violation of what God intends, but may even be cause for reexamining one's salvation. Human life is meant to be healthily social. So, too, is the spiritual life of a Christian.

We all need the church for a number of reasons. Among the more obvious are being able to worship God together, helping one another grow to spiritual maturity, and making an impact on the world. But we also need the church for other less obvious reasons.

First, we need the church for a sense of belonging. We were created by God to feel a need for being part of something greater than ourselves. There are other things that can fulfill that felt need in people, but a Christian needs to know that his life counts for Christ. That means he must have some connection with the church. The church is important to God, and a Christian will not be fully in step with the Lord until the church is also important to him. This gives the Christian a sense of belonging and purpose which, if everything in his life is in balance, will satisfy him as nothing else can.

We need the church; the church needs us.

Second, we need the church for greater safety. All too often, we see the church as an intrusive authority, and some churches have been guilty of being that. However, a mature, biblical church can function as a wonderfully reassuring source of guidance and protection. If we take to heart the message and life of a spiritually nurturing church, it will help us avoid sins that will hurt us, and provide encouragement that may help us keep from getting overcome by discouragement or temptation.

Third, we need the church for fellowship. We were not created to be able to make it alone. We need other people, and Christians need other Christians. Ephesians 4:12–16 makes it clear that only through mutual ministry, as members of the body of Christ commit themselves to the welfare of each other, can we all grow to maturity in Christ. We need to meet with others in the church on a regular basis (Hebrews 10:24–25), we need to participate in baptism (Matthew 28:19–20), communion (1 Corinthians 11:23–26), exercise church discipline (Hebrews 13:17; 1 Corinthians 5:13; Galatians 6:1), and sit under biblical preaching (Titus 1:3).

If the church is this important to us, then others in the church must need us too. We are the ones who make this contribution to them. The church also needs our time, our talents, and our treasures. Keeping the ministry of a church going requires massive contributions of time and talent from lay people. It also requires great commitment of treasures. Ministry that costs nothing accomplishes nothing. If we each give as the Lord has prospered us, the church will have little difficulty fulfilling the mandate given it in Scripture.

Speed Bump

Slow down to be sure you've gotten the main points from this chapter.

Question

Answer

Q1. How do I join the body?

A1. I join the body by becoming a *Christian*.

Q2. What is my gift to the body?

A2. My gift to the body is to use my *spiritual* gift in its behalf.

Q3. What is my Christian duty to the body?

A3. My duty is to *commit* myself to the body's welfare.

Fill in the Blank

Question
Answer

Q1. How do I join the body?

A1. I join the body by becoming a _____.

Q2. What is my gift to the body?

A2. My gift to the body is to use my _____ gift in its behalf.

Q3. What is my Christian duty to the body?

A3. My duty is to _____ myself to the body's welfare.

For Further Thought and Discussion

1. How important do you think it is for a local church to require a clear statement of personal salvation for membership? Why?

2. Do you know what your service gift might be to the body? Have you given your gift to the body? Have you benefited from the gifts of others in the body? How seriously have you taken your contribution to the body in the past? Why?

3. Have you done your Christian duty to the church? In some areas but not in others? What do you think you need to do to complete your duty to the church?

What If I Don't Believe?

If I don't believe in the importance of my contribution to the church, I will miss out on the blessing of giving to others, and others will suffer because they need what I am not giving them. Everyone loses.

For Further Study

1. Scripture

- Romans 12:6–8
- 1 Corinthians 12–14

- Galatians 6:10
- Ephesians 4:11–16
- 1 Peter 4:10

2. Books

The Walk, Gene Getz
The Purpose Driven Church, Rick Warren

Far from turning us away from the world,
Christ directs us to it. He awakens within us
an altogether new concern for it.

9

■ Paul Tournier—1898–1986

What Difference Should My Salvation Make to the World?

In his book, *The Body,* Chuck Colson tells the story of some young people from Shively Christian Church who, during summer Bible camp, were challenged by their pastor to go out and find some practical way to be servants.

The kids divided into groups, one of which did two hours of yard work for an elderly man. Another group bought ice cream treats for several widows in the church. Two other groups visited a church member in a hospital and sang Christmas carols at a nursing home (yes, in August!).

But everything changed when one group reported that they had gone to their rival neighbor, Shively Baptist, and asked the pastor if he knew of anyone who needed help. The pastor sent them to the home of an elderly woman who needed yard work done. There, for two hours, they mowed grass, raked the yard, and trimmed hedges.

When they were getting ready to leave, the woman called the group together and thanked them for their hard work. "I don't know how I could get along without you," she told them. "You kids at Shively Baptist are always coming to my rescue."

"Shively Baptist!" interrupted Pastor Stone. "I sure hope you set her straight and told her you were from Shively Christian Church."

"Why, no we didn't," the kids said. "We didn't think it mattered" (113).

This is a small example of a great truth. The world ought to always be a better place because a Christian has lived. When a person becomes a Christian, he should attempt, according to the leading of the Lord, to influence his world with kingdom character and kingdom principles. That is, he should act like a citizen of the kingdom of heaven, and he

should attempt, as much as he has opportunity, to influence his world
with kingdom of heaven principles.

In this chapter we learn that . . .

1. A Christian should help those in need who come across his path, and
   whose need he is able to meet.
2. A Christian should be a good citizen to help establish justice and
   righteousness in the nation.
3. A Christian should love his neighbor as himself.
4. A Christian should do his job as though he were working for Jesus.
5. A Christian should be a beacon of light to help make the world a better
   place in which to live.

The Bible teaches at least five areas where we have the opportunity and obligation to influence our world for the cause of Christ.
First, we should be a "good Samaritan" to those in need. Second, we
should be a good citizen of our nation. Third, we should be a good
neighbor to those around us. Fourth, we should be a good, faithful
worker. And finally, we should be a beacon of light to the world, thus
helping others to get an accurate picture of the God we serve.

What Is a Christian's Responsibility as a Good Samaritan?

*A Christian should help those in need who come across his path, and whose
need he is able to meet.*

Luke 10:25–37 tells of one day when Jesus was talking to a
group of people, and a lawyer asked Him what he had to do to
inherit eternal life. Jesus asked him what the Law said, and the
lawyer replied, "'You shall love the LORD your God with all your
heart, with all your soul, with all your strength, and with all your
mind,' and 'your neighbor as yourself,'" quoting Deuteronomy
6:5 and Leviticus 19:18. Jesus said that he was right. Then, wish-
ing to justify himself, the lawyer asked, "Who is my neighbor?"
In response, Jesus told the parable of the good Samaritan. A man
traveling on the road to Jericho was robbed, beaten, and left for
dead. A priest, and later a Levite, passed by but did nothing to
help their fellow Jew. Then a Samaritan, hated by the Jews,
passed by and helped him. Then Jesus asked, "So which of these

three do you think was neighbor to him who fell among the thieves?" The lawyer answered, "He who showed mercy on him." Jesus said, "Go and do likewise."

Why I Need to Know This

I need to know this so that I will respond to all my God-given responsibilities that lie outside the strictly "spiritual" realm. Sometimes we think that going to church and sharing our faith complete our Christian duty. These principles and passages make it clear that our responsibilities go much farther, and unless I know this, I may fail in these areas.

From this parable we learn several things. First, the man who was robbed was in trouble through no fault of his own. Second, the Samaritan's life path crossed his. Third, the Samaritan was able to help him. Fourth, he was therefore, according to Jesus, obligated to help. Whenever we come across people under the same sort of circumstances, we, too, are obligated to help them.

Of course, this principle has become harder to apply because modern media show us the suffering of many more people than we could possibly help. On television news or advertising we learn of the plights of refugees, orphans, disaster victims, and victims of war and civil strife by the thousands and tens of thousands. We cannot possibly help them all. As a result, it is all too easy to get callused and help no one. That, however, ignores the parable of the good Samaritan, which we are not at liberty to do.

I once heard the story of a young man who was on the beach early one morning where, the night before, thousands upon thousands of starfish had been washed upon the shore. He was throwing them back into the ocean, one at a time. Another man watched him for some time and then said to him, "Why are you bothering throwing the starfish back? There are so many of them, and you are able to help so few of them, it couldn't possibly matter." The young man looked at him, looked at the starfish in his hand, threw the starfish back into the ocean, and replied, "It matters to that one."

We can't help everyone, but we can help someone.

And so it is. We cannot possibly help everyone, but we can help someone. And it matters to that someone.

I will never forget the time the Lord was working in my life to rid me of the "since-I-can't-help-everyone-I-won't-help-anyone" syndrome. I was driving down a busy city street on a cold winter morning when I saw a young woman standing at an intersection with a cardboard sign that said: "NEED MONEY TO GET HOME. WILLING TO WORK." She was freezing. She had on a thin jacket that was not nearly enough to protect her from the biting cold. Her face was red. Her eyes were red and watering, and her nose was running. The expression on her face was altogether desperate.

I had been told that people who don't need the money, or who are unwilling to work, or who use money for drugs and booze often pull this scam. But something seemed different about this young woman. I thought, *This is a hard way to get money if you don't have to.* Yet, my practical nature reared up. *You don't know this woman. She might be a drug addict. If you help her, you will probably only be helping her support her irresponsibility. Besides, you have to be a good steward of your money, and not throw it down a rat hole.*

But another voice seemed to be speaking, too. It said, *Max, you find it a little too easy to dismiss these kinds of people by feigning ignorance. Are you really convinced these people are undeserving, or do you just want to save your time and money by ignoring them?*

By this time, the light had turned green and the traffic began moving. But I couldn't get the woman out of my mind. The combination of the fact that she seemed desperate, and was indeed suffering from the cold, along with my own willful ignorance of her situation, created in me a tremendous internal struggle. Suddenly, the issue was not just between the young lady and me; it was between God and me. I believe God used that experience to get my attention and make a decision as to whose money was in the bank, God's or mine. Whose time was I to allocate, God's or mine? Whose values was I to live out, God's or mine?

When I had run my errands, I drove back down that same road, and there she was, an hour later and an hour colder. I couldn't think of anything she could do for me for which I could pay her. So I drove to an automatic teller machine and withdrew $100. Then I drove back to where the girl was standing, pulled off to the side of the road, and began talking with her. She said she was going home to Phoenix to see her parents, whom she had not seen in a long time, and she ran out of money. She couldn't get a job, because all the places where she might work required a phone number. She had gotten food and shelter at the rescue mission downtown, but they could not help her get home.

I still don't know if she was telling the truth, but if she was not, she was paying a terrible price for the lie. So the issue before me was whether or not I was willing to not give her money and risk the possibility that she was telling the truth, or give her money and risk the possibility that she was lying to me. God made it clear that I was to give her the money. I told her, "I don't know if you are telling me the truth or not, but I am going to give you $100. This will get you a bus ticket to Phoenix and get you something to eat along the way. But I want you to know why I am giving you the money. A number of years ago, I committed my life to **We serve others in Jesus' name.** Christ, to try to live as He would want me to. I want you to know that I am giving you this money in the name of Jesus."

Well, if she wasn't a mess before, she became a real mess then. She started bawling, and her nose started running worse. It wasn't a pretty sight. But I drove away feeling good about two things. One, if she was telling the truth, I had helped a person in real need. Second, God had gotten a hold on my heart, and it gave me a sense of freedom.

I have not helped everyone that I have seen in similar situations since that day. I can't. I don't have that much money. But now, because the Lord knows I am willing, He has directed me to help those He wants me to help. And while I can't help everyone, I can help the ones the Lord brings across my path, whose need is real, and whose need I can meet.

If we all accepted our responsibility to be good Samaritans, we would be stronger, freer Christians for it, and much suffering would be relieved in this fallen world.

What Is a Christian's Responsibility as a Good Citizen?

A Christian should be a good citizen to help establish justice and righteousness in the nation.

Each Christian has citizenship in some country, and those of us in the United States are particularly privileged. We are the most prosperous and powerful nation on earth, and our people may enjoy more freedoms and opportunities than any others.

The Bible speaks clearly to us in our roles as citizens of the U.S. Romans 13:1–7 and 1 Peter 2:13–17 tell us that we are to be subject to the governing authorities over us because they are appointed by God. This, however, must be balanced with other Scripture that tells us we are free to disobey whenever the government asks us to do something that is contrary to God's word (Acts 4:19–21).

In addition, because of our unique position as citizens of a nation governed by laws ratified by the people, we have an opportunity, and therefore an obligation, to help establish justice and righteousness in our nation. The foundation for this assertion lies in the Old Testament. Throughout the life of Israel as a nation, the kings were called upon by God to establish "justice and righteousness in the land" (2 Samuel 8:15; 1 Kings 10:9; Psalm 89:14; Psalm 106:3; Proverbs 21:3). These were the primary characteristics God was looking for in a monarchy, and things that God loves. God evaluated each reign by these criteria.

We are not kings, and we do not live in a monarchy. But as citizens of a nation that elects those who will serve in government, we are responsible to help elect those who will be most likely to establish justice and righteousness in the land. That means that our criteria for voting should not be primarily speaking ability, or good looks, or economic policy, but rather the degree to which the person's policies would foster justice and righteousness.

We must exert a positive influence on our nation. Of course, this does not mean that we should elect someone who might be good at fostering justice and righteousness but inept at governing. Rather, it means that we must vote for, and if necessary encourage to run (or run ourselves), those who are qualified to govern and who would do so in a way to promote justice and righteousness.

What Is a Christian's Responsibility as a Good Neighbor?

A Christian should love his neighbor as himself.

The apostle Paul states this principle as clearly as it can be stated: "For all the law is fulfilled in one word, even in this: 'You shall love your neighbor as yourself'" (Galatians 5:14). This means that the people with whom we come in contact in the normal course of living our lives are to be treated as we would like to be treated. Jesus said it clearly in what is known as the "golden rule": "Do to others as you would have them do to you" (Luke 6:31, NIV). This includes our physical neighbors, but goes far beyond them. It includes our families, our fellow churchgoers, the people we encounter in the living of our lives (grocery store, gas station, doctor's office, school, etc.). If we would not like to be spoken to impolitely, then we should not speak impolitely. If we would not like to be cut in front of while waiting in line, then we should not cut in front of others. If we would not like to be gossiped about, taken advantage of, treated disrespectfully, or cheated out of money, then we most certainly should not do those things either.

On the other hand, if we would like to be spoken to politely, have people be friendly to us, have people look out for us, help us in need, and hold us in high esteem, then we should do so to others. This is what it means to be a good neighbor.

We could cite an infinite number of examples of love, some of them heroic and some of them utterly simple and mundane. Because life consists more of the mundane than the heroic, I want to share the story of a husband who was asked the secret of his successful 50-year marriage. He replied that his wife, Sarah, was the only girl he had ever dated. After their wedding, Sarah's father got him alone and gave him a box which, he said, contained the secret of a happy marriage. The young groom opened the package to find a large, gold watch. Across the face of it, where he would see it many times a day, were etched the words, "Say something nice to Sarah."

The spirit of this gift, if applied to every area and every person of our lives, would bring great success. It would help us to love our neighbor.

What Is a Christian's Responsibility as a Good Worker?

A Christian should do his job as though he were working for Jesus.

A Christian should do his job as though he were working for Jesus because that is the case. Colossians 3:22–24 says,

Slaves, obey your earthly masters in everything; and do it, not only when their eye is on you and to win their favor, but with sincerity of heart and reverence for the Lord. Whatever you do, work at it with all your heart, as working for the Lord, not for men, since you know that you will receive an inheritance from the Lord as a reward. It is the Lord Christ you are serving (NIV).

There are four crucial elements we must include if we are to do our job as unto Christ.

1. Excellence. We must do our job as well as we can. That does not mean we must do it as well as someone else, because that other person may not be able to do it as well as we can, in which case we would be doing less than our best for the Lord. But on the other hand, the other person may be able to do our job better than we can, and if we hold ourselves to his standard of performance, it may drive us to frustration and defeat. Instead, we should do a ruthless evaluation of our abilities and give ourselves to the Lord, in confidence and comfort, to do our job as well as we can. With that, the Lord is pleased.

2. Respect. Our fellow-workers, those in authority over us, those under us, companies that supply us, and customers all **Our best work** must be treated with dignity and respect. To do **honors Christ.** less is to dishonor Christ in our job.

3. Morality. We must be honest, ethical, and moral in all we do. We must be trusted because of our track record. We must never steal from our employer, neither actual goods, nor time that we steal by falsifying how long we work or by being lazy and inefficient. We also must be upright in our dealings with co-workers and ethical with any suppliers or customers.

4. Trust. We must trust all results in the workplace to God. The workplace is not always fair or kind. We may be overlooked for a promotion because of insider-manipulations, or we may not be paid what we should be paid by industry standards, or a woman may not get paid as much as a man doing the same job, or one in a minority group may get overlooked in promotions. A boss may have it in for us. The world did not treat our Lord fairly, and it should come as no surprise that we may also get treated unfairly.

This does not mean, of course, that we cannot change jobs if it is in the will of God. We are not slaves, and if it seems best to change jobs, and the Lord allows that to happen, there is nothing wrong with it. It just means that while we are in the workplace, we must work as unto Christ, even when conditions are not perfect.

A person recently told me how badly his job was going. He got no respect from his supervisor, they did not give him the pay raises they promised when they hired him, and they made him work unreasonable hours without overtime pay. The man was livid. He said that he was going to look for another job, and while he was looking, he was going to try to do whatever he could to slow down production and lose the company money. "I'll teach them to mess with me," was his attitude. It is understandable. It is natural. But it is not right. We serve Christ first, our employer second.

What Is a Christian's Responsibility as a Beacon of Light?

A Christian should be a beacon of light to help make the world a better place in which to live.

No one questions that the world in which we live is facing serious problems. Among many complicated and intertwining reasons, one is that many areas of society have been abandoned by Christians. Not surprisingly, as a result those areas have become almost totally secularized. The areas of education, the arts and entertainment, and the media, among others, have become strongholds of secular values, pulling down the civilization that was built to greatness on biblical principles.

Why did we abandon these areas? One reason may be that we have had a "sinking ship" mentality. Since many Christians believed that Christ was coming back soon, they concluded that working for the good of this world was a waste of time, like rearranging the deck chairs on the *Titanic*. The ship is going down, was the thought, so the only legitimate activity is to get people into the lifeboats.

It is certainly true that the ship is going down, but we don't know when, and we may have to live many years yet on the ship before it sinks. Since the world has not ended as soon as many thought it would, we are left to live in a world that is increasingly hostile to our beliefs, and increasingly gaining the upper hand in laws and public attitudes. We face a bad situation which in some

Christians must reenter the culture wars.

measure is of our own making. Now we have to play catch-up. We must try to reclaim ground that was lost unnecessarily. We must try to reassert kingdom principles in all areas of life in which we have influence. We should try to create beauty and goodness wherever the Lord gives us opportunity and His leading.

This should include all areas that are not illegal or immoral. For example, when God wanted to build a building that would reflect Him in the Old Testament, He chose artisans who were as skilled as any in the world. They knew how to create beauty, and they did it. Solomon's temple was one of the most glorious buildings ever constructed. But what if none of God's people had believed that beauty was important? What if God could find no one to construct a building according to His specifications? Then the glory of God on earth would have been diminished.

We are living, in America, in a day when goodness and beauty are disappearing. Television, music, movies, and literature glorify sex, drugs, violence, self-gratification, self-mutilation, and death. We are seeing more that reflects ugliness and evil than beauty and goodness.

Christians must no longer disassociate themselves from intercourse with culture. We must no longer leave our society and culture to those who advance ugliness and evil. We must advance beauty and goodness wherever we are able. This can mean something as simple as a homemaker planting a flowerbed, or a Christian artist creating and performing, if she is able, the best music in the world. If she is not able to create and perform on that level, at least we can stop imitating the world's idea of excellence and create and perform that which seems good in the eyes of God.

This same principle applies in many areas beyond the field of art. It applies to all areas. Many Christians have largely pulled

Jesus called His followers to be salt and light.

out of leadership and effective participation in PTAs, service groups, and boards of community agencies. We have left those things to the world, and as a result, the world has created them after their own image. We need to be good artists, teachers, homemakers, mechanics, or whatever our vocation to the glory of

God. We need to be beacons of light, set on a hill, so that the kingdom principles we are advancing will have an opportunity to penetrate the world in which we live. Furthermore, the world needs to see our good works and glorify our Father who is in heaven (Matthew 14—16).

Conclusion

We began this chapter by saying that the world should always be a little bit better place because a Christian has lived, and the remainder of the chapter specified ways and areas in which this could be done. Each Christian is responsible, I believe, to embrace this principle. However, we must be comfortable with the differences in opportunity and capacity that God has given each of us. That is, a world-class evangelist or entertainer has been given greater capacity than most of us to impact the world. People you know personally have been given greater capacities in some areas than you have.

This is due to the sovereignty of God, however, and those of us who are less gifted need not feel inferior or inadequate because we cannot serve the Lord with as much result as these people. We are to fulfill our mandate as God has enabled us, not as He has enabled others.

On the other hand, no believer should use this as an excuse for doing nothing. Just because we cannot do something as well as someone else does not mean we cannot do anything. So we minister within the range of gifts, abilities, circumstances, and blessings that God gives us, content in the knowledge that God does not reward results but faithfulness. In that regard, we are all on an equal footing. We can all be equally faithful to what God asks of us.

Speed Bump

Slow down to be sure you've gotten the main points of this chapter.

Question **A**nswer

Q1. What is a Christian's responsibility as a good Samaritan?

A1. A Christian should help those in *need* who come across his path, and whose need he is able to meet.

Q2. What is a Christian's responsibility as a good citizen?

A2. A Christian should be a good citizen to help establish justice and *righteousness* in the nation.

Q3. What is a Christian's responsibility as a good neighbor?

A3. A Christian should *love* his neighbor as himself.

Q4. What is a Christian's responsibility as a good worker?

A4. A Christian should do his job as though he were working for *Jesus*.

Q5. What is a Christian's responsibility as a beacon of light?

A5. A Christian should be a beacon of light to help make the world a *better* place in which to live.

Fill in the Blank

Q uestion
A nswer

Q1. What is a Christian's responsibility as a good Samaritan?

A1. A Christian should help those in _____ who come across his path, and whose need he is able to meet.

Q2. What is a Christian's responsibility as a good citizen?

A2. A Christian should be a good citizen to help establish justice and _____ in the nation.

Q3. What is a Christian's responsibility as a good neighbor?

A3. A Christian should _____ his neighbor as himself.

Q4. What is a Christian's responsibility as a good worker?

A4. A Christian should do his job as though he were working for

_____.

Q5. What is a Christian's responsibility as a beacon of light?

A5. A Christian should be a beacon of light to help make the world a _____ place in which to live.

For Further Thought and Discussion

1. What has been your attitude toward those in need around you? Do you help them? How do you think Christians/the church can do a better job of identifying those who really need help?

2. How seriously have you taken your responsibility as a good citizen in the past? Have you voted faithfully? Have you voted for those you thought would be most qualified to help establish justice and righteousness in the nation? Has your perspective toward being a good citizen changed as a result of this chapter? If so, how?

3. What do you think is one thing you can begin doing to be a better neighbor to others?

4. What is the area that needs the most attention from you in being a good worker? What can you do to be a better worker?

5. What do you consider the most important area of being a beacon of light to your world? How do you think you can be a beacon of light in that area?

What If I Don't Believe?

If I don't believe that I have these responsibilities, I will fail to live up to major expectations that the Lord has of me, and I will contribute to the overall decline in quality of life in America because of my passivity. I will be a poor example to my children or to others, possibly encouraging them to be passive.

For Further Study

1. Scripture

- 2 Samuel 8:15
- Matthew 5:14–16
- Luke 10:25–37
- Romans 13:1–7
- 1 Corinthians 5:9–10
- Galatians 5:17

- Colossians 3:22–24
- 1 Peter 2:13–17

2. Books

Your Work Matters to God, Doug Sherman
A Dangerous Grace, Charles Colson
Winning the Values War, Leith Anderson
Halftime, Bob Buford

*Great works do not always lie in our way, but
every moment we may do little ones
excellently, that is, with great love.*
■ Saint Francis of Sales (1567–1622)

What Is the Way Things Are Supposed to Be?

I read a story one time—just one small example of the way things are supposed to be. Gail Blank wrote of a day when she and her husband drove to a country orchard to pick fresh peaches. They drove to a sign that said, "Peaches-U-Pick—3 mi." They turned down a dirt road to another sign and arrow: "Peaches." They wound their way far back off the road to a remote spot where there was a wooden table, a little trailer, three dogs, several cats, and nothing but peach trees as far as the eye could see. No one seemed to be around, however. There was a sign on the table that said, "Welcome, friends. Peaches are $5.00 per basket. Pick all you want. Then put the money in the slot below. Have fun."

"How do you know where to start?" my husband asked.

"Well," I said loudly, looking at the dogs, "do you guys wanna pick peaches?" They started barking and bouncing around, then raced off ahead. It was pretty obvious what the routine was here.

We followed the dogs to a grove where the trees were loaded with beautiful ripe fruit. I ran to one tree, my husband to another, each of us followed by a canine companion. When our baskets were full, we headed back, our new friends leading the way (Gainsville *Sun*, April, 19, 1996).

They paid for their fruit and began to drive out. As they did, another car drove in. Gail watched the new visitor as he read the directions on the poster. Then he too picked up a basket and followed the barking, bounding dogs to the orchard. As Gail and her husband drove off slowly, they looked back on a simple place of pure enjoyment.

When I read that story, silly as it may seem, I got a lump in my throat because I thought to myself, *that's the way things are supposed to be!* People are supposed to be able to work hard and grow peaches.

Then they are supposed to be able to put up a sign and trust people to pay for the peaches they pick. Dogs are supposed to wag their tails and be friendly and lead people where they want to go. It was a simple little story that will never make any great contribution to the world. But it gives us a tiny little glimpse of the way things are supposed to be.

In this chapter we learn that . . .

1. Shalom means not just an absence of conflict, but the presence of all things as they should be.
2. Today, shalom is thwarted by sin.
3. We can encourage shalom by trying to live life as Jesus would if He were in our shoes.

In his book *Not the Way Things Are Supposed to Be,* Cornelius Plantinga recounted the story of a man in a large city who was caught in a traffic jam on a main road, so he exited and tried to make better time on side streets. It was night, and he soon became lost on streets that narrowed and became darker and more deserted. Finally, the unthinkable happened. His expensive car stalled on a dark, dangerous street ruled by teenaged thugs. He called a tow truck with his cellular phone, but before it arrived, the gang members surrounded his car and threatened to beat him up and possibly kill him. Just at the last moment, the tow truck drove up and the driver confronted the gang members:

Man, the world ain't supposed to work like this. Maybe you don't know that, but this ain't the way it's supposed to be. I'm supposed to be able to do my job without askin' you if I can. And that dude is supposed to be able to wait with his car without you rippin' him off. Everything's supposed to be different than what it is here (7).

And so it is. Everything is supposed to be much different than we commonly see it. So how is the way things are supposed to be? And how can we as Christians—those who have received salvation—help make the world more like it is supposed to be?

What Does Shalom Mean?

Shalom means not just an absence of conflict, but the presence of all things as they should be.

The word *shalom* is a Hebrew word that means "peace." However, it means more than an absence of war, or an absence of interpersonal conflict or internal emotional turmoil. Rather than meaning only the absence of negative things, it also includes the presence of positive things.

In the Bible, shalom means universal flourishing, wholeness, and delight—a rich state of affairs in which natural needs are satisfied and natural gifts fruitfully employed, a state of affairs that inspires joyful wonder as its Creator and Savior opens doors and welcomes the creatures in whom he delights (Plantinga, 10).

In God's original creation, shalom was in full flower. The earth was kind to Adam and Eve. It yielded its fruit without fail. There were no earthquakes, floods, or famines. There was no interpersonal conflict. There was full, unbroken fellowship between human and human and between humans and God. Whatever was good was present. Whatever was bad was absent. That was shalom.

Why I Need to Know This

I need to know this so that I can contribute to the creation of partial shalom on earth now, as well as to look forward to complete shalom in heaven. I can help make the world a better place in which to live and take great meaning from investing my life in such a worthy purpose. In addition, I can draw joy and strength from the hope that is offered by the promise of complete, unending shalom in heaven.

But perfect shalom was lost by sin. The end came when Adam and Eve took things into their own hands, rebelled against God, and ate of the tree of the knowledge of good and evil—the only thing in the entire world they had been forbidden to do. Afterward, there was estrangement between humans and God. God used to walk in the cool of the evening with Adam and Eve, talking with them face to face. After Adam and Eve sinned, they hid from God. They said they hid because they were naked. When God asked Adam if he had eaten from the forbidden tree, Adam tried to blame God for it ("The woman *whom You gave*" me caused the problem, Genesis 3:12).

Now many people have turned their backs on God. Many do not believe in Him. Of those who believe in Him, many do not worship Him. Of those who worship Him, many do not obey Him. Perfect shalom has been broken.

There also was estrangement between human and human. When God asked Adam what had happened, Adam also tried to blame Eve (*"The woman* whom you gave to be with me, she gave me of the tree, and I ate," Genesis 3:12). In addition, there was now a power struggle between man and woman (Genesis 3:16), each one wanting the upper hand in the relationship.

Today, homes are broken. Children are abused. Business people try to take advantage of consumers and consumers shoplift from businesses. Politicians lie. Ministers cheat. Workers steal.

Sin causes estrangement, destroying shalom. The law of the jungle struggles to become the law of the land: the survival of the fittest, where people see other people either as commodities to be used in the pursuit of their personal goals or as obstacles, when they get in the way. Perfect shalom between people has been broken.

There was also estrangement between humans and creation. After the Great Rebellion, the earth no longer readily fed Adam and Eve. It fought them. The ground was cursed (Genesis 3:18–19). Now there are earthquakes, floods, droughts, diseases, and all kinds of natural disasters in which creation wreaks havoc on humanity. And in return, humanity wreaks havoc on creation, poisoning the air and water, ruining the soil, and denuding the forests. Perfect shalom has been broken.

Perfect shalom is no more. It is a fallen world.

How Is Shalom Thwarted Today?

Today, shalom is thwarted by sin.

Perfect shalom was broken by sin in the garden of Eden, and that cataclysm has its continuing effect today. Bad things still happen that are beyond anyone's control. Children are still born with birth defects. Volcanoes still erupt. The earth still quakes. Rivers still flood, and winds still blow.

But there is a level of shalom that can be encouraged or discouraged by how we act. It is this controllable shalom that is thwarted by sin. By the sins of attack we vandalize shalom, and by the sins of flight we abandon it. In either case, shalom is thwarted.

A husband works seventy hours a week. He is disengaged from his family. His time with his wife is limited to eating and sleeping. His time with his children is less than that. He provides no emotional or spiritual leadership in the family. His children are more influenced by their peer group than by their father. They are falling into self-destructive behavior. He ignores them or yells at them. His wife feels alone. Shalom is destroyed.

A salesperson checks into a hotel, flips on the cable TV and watches a racy movie, then drops off to sleep. Though he is married, he flirts with the hotel desk clerk, and later with the secretary of the person he is meeting, and after that the flight attendants. Back in his office, he pads his expense account. Shalom is destroyed.

A single mother is desperate to get married. She needs more money to get her child out of a third-rate day-care center. She is a Christian, but willingly encourages the advances of a non-Christian man in the office about whom she knows very little. She hopes that something will work out, and if they get married and it doesn't work out, she may be able to get alimony from him. Shalom is destroyed.

Two stay-at-home moms meet for lunch. They stick the kids in the family room with baloney sandwiches and a Disney video. They **How we act affects shalom.** sit at the kitchen table and gossip about their friend who is having marital problems. They cut her down and laugh at her misfortune, blaming it on her own inadequacies. Shalom is destroyed.

A husband is irritated with his wife's appearance. When they first married, she was attractive. Now, three children later, she looks older than he does. It embarrasses him. He rides her to lose weight and take better care of herself. His anger is always just below the surface, and he browbeats her with unrealistic expectations. Shalom is destroyed.

A teenage boy talks a girl he doesn't even like very well into going to bed with him. He tells her he loves her and wants to marry her. He tells her he will always be there for her. She consents. He drops her the next day, and tells all his friends about it. Shalom is destroyed.

A mother tells her daughter, who has a pretty voice, that she ought to stop kidding herself about singing and start thinking about something that will earn her a living. Shalom is destroyed.

A teacher has a run-in with a student. The student is aggressive and rude. Shalom is destroyed. Later, the student completes an exam with several essay questions on it. The teacher fails him, when the answers, while not great, were good enough to pass. More shalom is destroyed.

Example after example could be given. The point is that all sin destroys shalom. The sin may be something we shouldn't do that we do, or it may be something we should do that we don't. We may fall short of an ideal, or we may transgress a law. Both are sin.

We are to love God with all our hearts and souls and mind, and we are to love our neighbor as ourselves (Matthew 22:37–43). Loving God means that we obey Him (John 15:10). Loving our neighbor means that we help those in need if we are able, and that we are patient and kind, not envious, self-exalted, rude, or easily provoked (1 Corinthians 13:4–7). Anything short of this kind of love destroys shalom.

How Can We Help Restore Shalom?

We can encourage shalom by trying to live life as Jesus would if He were in our shoes.

Sin destroys shalom. Righteousness allows shalom to be restored—partially on earth, and completely and forever in heaven. Even in a fallen world, we can nurture, foster, and encourage shalom. Perfect shalom will not be seen again on this earth as we know it, but a restoration of partial shalom lies within the power of each of us. We encourage shalom by trying to do what is right and good in every situation in life, and encouraging others by word and deed to do the same.

Aaron Feuerstein helped restore shalom when fire swept through his textile mills in Lawrence, Massachusetts, one cold December night. Those mills provided jobs for over 3,000 people throughout the Northeast, and provided the nation with much of its supply of Polartec, a popular winter fabric used in serious outdoor clothing. The workers were stunned. Their livelihoods were eliminated. They were ruined—they thought!

Feuerstein flew to the site the next day. More than 1,000 workers were gathered in the office building as he came in. A hush fell over the crowd. "When all the textile mills in Lawrence (Massachusetts) ran out to get cheaper labor down south, we stuck," he shouted. "We're going to stay—and rebuild."

The workers could not believe their ears. They erupted in jubilation. But privately, many of the workers doubted that it could be done soon enough to help them. They assumed it would take many months to get the plant up and running again.

> **We encourage shalom when we do what is right and good.**

Later, Feuerstein met with his engineers. "I want to be up and running in a week," he told them.

"Impossible!" was the reply from the head engineer. Four weeks would be the earliest, and that was questionable.

"You're the best engineer in the world. You'll figure it out," rejoined Feuerstein calmly.

Wages for the hourly workers were due in two weeks. Instructions were given to pay everyone in full, and give a Christmas bonus. The workers were stunned. Many of them thought they had already seen the last money from the mills. Along with the bonus was a note written by Feuerstein: "Do not despair. God bless each of you."

Then, on the third day after the fire, he met with worried employees and announced that for the next 30 days—and longer, if necessary—all employees would be paid full salaries. Workers cheered. Then Feuerstein added, "By January 2, we will restart operations."

Now there was pandemonium. Men pumped their fists in the air. Women burst into tears. "When you work for Aaron," someone shouted, "you're *somebody!*"

Seven days after the fire, on December 18, the first machine started up in the Polartec building. Four days later, part of a production line began running. Twenty-two days after the fire, 300 other workers reported for duty. The people responsible for getting the machinery up and running were being called the Dream Team.

To prove to customers that his mills were back into production, Feuerstein flew to a trade show in Nevada and there, via a satellite hook-up, let everyone see the mills running. They were able to fill 80 percent of their orders already. "My workers have accomplished a miracle," he told his customers. It was like family members work-

> **Shalom is not just personal—it affects all who are around us.**

ing together, each one doing what he could for the good of the whole. Feuerstein had met adversity with courage, ingenuity, and loyalty.

To anyone who understands the real obstacles involved, this positive outcome seems virtually impossible. Yet it happened. Why? Because one man cared deeply about his workers, his customers, and the reputation of his family name. One man helped restore shalom not only for the 3,000 people depending on him, but also the other millions who learned of his vision and courage.

On a much smaller, more intimate scale, Mike Powell helped restore shalom for his six brothers and sisters. When his mother, who was a drug addict, moved out with one of her boyfriends, Mike, who was only fifteen years old, kept them together, found a place for them to live, and kept them clean, fed, and in school against the greatest of odds. Yet his luck began to run out. One day there was no food left. Michelle, the youngest, was crying from hunger, and Mike had run out of options. There was nothing he knew to do. All night, he rocked the hungry baby and prayed for help.

Help came on Thanksgiving Day. As Mike was walking along a street, he passed a church group offering free food for the needy. The volunteers were skeptical that Mike would need a dozen sandwiches, but they finally gave them to him anyway. Later, he returned with the children to prove he was telling the truth. The church volunteers were so impressed with him and his polite siblings that they began asking questions. Mike finally told them about all the years he had been caring for his brothers and sisters.

The church helped him temporarily, but could not find a foster home where all seven children could go. Mike insisted that the family be kept together, and the only place he knew where that might be done was at his grandmother and grandfather's home. Up until this time, he had kept his desperate situation from them, trying to cover up for his derelict mother. But his grandparents insisted the children stay with them. They even moved, so that the kids could have a house to live in instead of an apartment, and a yard to play in.

Now Mike is dedicated to reaching inner-city youngsters, but his greatest satisfaction is in knowing that his siblings are thriving. Mike helped restore shalom for his family.

The examples are as endless as the people on earth and the experiences they have. When we speak kindly to our spouse who has had a rough day and didn't get everything done he or she should have, we foster shalom. When we give part of our income to further the gospel of Christ on earth, we foster shalom. When we decide not to retaliate against a person who has spoken rudely to us, or to let it go when someone takes credit for something we did at work, or to return money from an overpayment made to us by an insurance company, we foster shalom.

We can all help restore shalom to people. It can be as simple as smiling and being gracious to a grocery-store check-out clerk who has made a mistake on your bill. Or it can be as great as a medical researcher finding a cure for cancer. But our salvation should cause us not only to want to take the message of eternal salvation to others who might otherwise miss it, but it should cause us to want to help foster, nurture, and expand the characteristics of heaven while still here on earth (James 4:17). We should try, as much as we are able, to help make things the way they are supposed to be.

A smile or a kind word can foster shalom.

Conclusion

The negative impact of sin should be balanced by an awareness of the grace of God. We should be comforted by the knowledge that God wants shalom and is willing to pay any price to restore it. Human sin is relentless, but not as relentless as the grace of God. To speak of sin without grace is to minimize the resurrection of Jesus and the power of the Holy Spirit within the human heart.

But to speak of grace without sin is also a mistake. If we do not speak of sin as clearly as the Bible does, we trivialize the cross of Christ. The grace of God comes to us, as Plantinga states, with blood on it. Why would God leave the glories of heaven and come to earth? Why would He endure the humiliation of humans who spit on Him and beat Him, when all the while He could have annihilated them with a word? Why would a holy God allow the sin of the world to be placed on Him—an experience that surely aroused more revulsion and pain than any experience a human could imagine? Would He have endured that for nothing?

We must speak of sin and grace together.

To speak of grace, without at the same time owning up to our own sin and the part it played in driving the nails into Jesus, is to reduce grace to a heroic example of sacrifice. It is that, but it is much more. Without Jesus' death, our sins could never have been forgiven. Without His resurrection, we could never have our own resurrection.

It is popular now to speak of self-esteem and positive thinking as being the heart of salvation. It is popular now for churches to provide "seeker sensitive" services, so that unbelievers are not unnecessarily turned off by traditional worship services. Perhaps these things can be used to help create shalom if they are properly integrated with the rest of truth. However, for the Christian church to "ignore, euphemize, or otherwise mute the lethal reality of sin," Plantinga says insightfully, "is to cut the nerve of the gospel" (199).

We must acknowledge the reality of sin in our lives. It is sin and sin alone that separates us from God. It is sin and sin alone that needs to be remedied in order for us to be saved. It is our sin that Jesus came to die for. It is our sin that corrupts our present walk with God. It is sin that destroys shalom in our own lives today, just as in the Garden of Eden. Not until sin is done away with can shalom be fully restored.

And, the cold truth is that, unless we call sin sin—unless we accurately describe the centrality of it to the human experience, and unless we understand and communicate that Jesus Christ has come to save sinners and that without forgiveness of our sin, we will never be saved—then the gospel of grace becomes unnecessary, uninteresting, and ultimately an offense. We then need only the gospel of self-esteem, or self-help, or good works, or humanitarianism. To speak of the blood of Christ becomes distasteful and out of place. When the tax collector cried out, "God, be merciful to me a sinner," he had it right. And, he went home justified (Luke 18:13–14)—lifted up and not trodden down, cleansed and no longer guilty. By admitting our sin to God we can be rid of it. When we refuse to admit it, we must haul it around.

Speed Bump

Slow down to be sure you've gotten the main points from this chapter.

Question   **Q1.** What does shalom mean?

Answer   **A1.** Shalom means not just an absence of conflict, but the *presence* of all things as they should be.

Q2. How is shalom thwarted today?

A2. Today, shalom is thwarted by *sin.*

Q3. How can we help restore shalom?

A3. We can encourage shalom by trying to live life as *Jesus* would if He were in our shoes.

Fill in the Blank

Question   **Q1.** What does shalom mean?

Answer   **A1.** Shalom means not just an absence of conflict, but the _____ of all things as they should be.

Q2. How is shalom thwarted today?

A2. Today, shalom is thwarted by _____.

Q3. How can we help restore shalom?

A3. We can encourage shalom by trying to live life as _____ would if He were in our shoes.

For Further Thought and Discussion

1. If you were to describe a world as perfect as it can be (in light of the fact that we live in a fallen world), what would that world look like?

2. What do you think keeps the world from being like that?

3. What can you do to help make the world more like it should be? What can all Christians do?

What If I Don't Believe?

If I don't believe, I will not have as complete a vision of how the world can be as I should. As a result, I may not do as much as I could (and as much as the Lord wants me to) to help create shalom in my sphere of influence.

For Further Study

1. Scripture

- Genesis 3:1–24
- Matthew 22:37–41
- John 15:10
- 1 Corinthians 13:4–7
- James 4:17

2. Books

Not the Way It's Supposed to Be, Cornelius Plantinga, Jr.

Grace is love that cares and stoops and rescues.
■ John Stott

How Amazing Is Grace?

Many years ago, a new friend of mine took me to a country club to which he belonged. I knew little about country clubs. It was a stunningly beautiful place. The clubhouse, a huge mansion-like building, was set among large shade trees on a huge blanket of flawless grass. Behind the clubhouse were hundreds of acres of manicured golf greens, sloping gently down to a large river in the distance. While I didn't know the other gentleman well, I had been to his house, seen the cars he drove, observed his lifestyle in general, and did not expect him to be a member of such an exclusive club. I knew that it cost tens of thousands of dollars to join, and then on top of that you had to pay the monthly fees. I was mulling this over as we were seated near windows in the restaurant that overlooked the rolling, tree-dotted wonderland below.

The job he held as president of a large company paid him a generous but not lavish salary. As a bonus they threw in membership at the country club, which included a certain number of meals and rounds of golf each month. He could eat the allotted number of meals and play the allotted number of golf free each month. But unused meals and rounds of golf didn't carry over to the next month. If he didn't eat there often enough, or play enough golf in a given month, the benefits just went to waste.

So when, in ignorance of these facts, I offered to pay for my share of the meal, he replied, "Your money's no good here. You can't pay for anything. It's already paid for." And he meant it, literally. There were no cashiers, no cash registers, no one to take money. The member simply signed a statement and went on his way.

I thought how like membership in the body of Christ that was. Just as my friend could not afford to join the country club—the only way he could get it was to accept the membership as a gift when he accepted his job—so we cannot afford to buy our way into the body of

Christ. The only way we can get in is to receive it as a gift when we commit our lives to Christ. And once in, we cannot pay for the ongoing benefits. They have already been paid for. Yet, we often want to try to help pay for our membership into the body of Christ by being good people or by doing good works. And we often fear losing our membership if we are not good enough, or don't do enough good works.

In this chapter we learn that . . .

1. Grace is God's acceptance of you and blessing on you, even though you have not earned it.
2. Grace is necessary because we cannot be good enough to earn our salvation.
3. Grace costs the believer his pride and cost Jesus His life.
4. The result of grace is that we are completely accepted by God.
5. Our response to God's grace should be gratitude, obedience, and joy.

However, what if my friend were not content to accept the free gift of his country club membership? Imagine that he kept sending in money to the club for his membership. What a waste of money that would be. The membership was already paid for, and all he would be doing is needlessly draining his own resources.

That is the meaning, the essence of grace. We get what we get from God as a gift. We cannot pay for it, and it only drains us when we try. Until we learn how amazing God's grace is, we will never enter fully into the joy God intends us to have.

What Is Grace?

Grace is God's acceptance of you and blessing on you, even though you have not earned it.

Philip Yancey relates an incident that highlights the meaning and significance of grace.

During a British conference on comparative religions, experts from around the world debated what, if any, belief was unique to the Christian faith. They began eliminating possibilities. Incarnation? Other religions had different versions of gods appearing in human form. Resurrection? Again, other religions had accounts of return from death. The debate went on for some time until C. S. Lewis wandered into the room.

"What's the rumpus about?" he asked, and heard in reply that his colleagues were discussing Christianity's unique contribution among the world religions. Lewis responded, "Oh, that's easy. It's grace."

After some discussion, the conferees had to agree. The notion of God's love coming to us free of charge, no strings attached, seems to go against every instinct of humanity. The Buddhist eight-fold path, the Hindu doctrine of karma, the Jewish covenant, the Muslim code of law—each of these offers a way to earn approval. Only Christianity dares to make God's love unconditional (*What's So Amazing about Grace?* 45).

Primarily, grace means "unmerited favor" or "undeserved favor." It refers to the decision of God to bless you even though, on your own, you warrant His curse because of sin. But God loves you, so He has provided a way for you to be spared the normal consequence of sin, which is spiritual death and separation from God.

The Bible teaches us that the salvation we have in Jesus is not given to us because of our good works. Romans 11:6 says, "If [salvation] is by grace, it is no longer on the basis of works, otherwise grace is no longer grace" (NASB). Titus 3:5 says, "Not by works of righteousness which we have done, but according to His mercy He saved us, through the washing of regeneration and renewing of the Holy Spirit." So this salvation which we have in Jesus is not something we earn by being good or by doing good. It is something that is given to us by God's grace when we exercise faith in Jesus. He just does it because He wants to.

Why I Need to Know This

I need to know this so that I can understand the amazing benefits of God's grace, and fully experience the joy in the Lord, the strength available in trials, and the confidence to share my faith with others. When I understand how completely I am accepted in Christ, how totally I "belong" to God and His church, when I understand that God's grace is greater than all my sin, only then am I in a position to experience the fullness of life God has for me.

I read a story one time of two brothers who were both baseball card collectors. Whenever there was a little extra money on hand, down to the store they went, each to buy a pack of cards and hope to find the special one they wanted. The younger brother got the card the older one wanted. Used to trading, the older brother asked, "What do you want for it?" prepared to trade virtually his whole collection for it if necessary.

The younger brother looked at the card, shrugged his shoulders, and said, "You can have it."

Some time later, the older brother got the special card the younger brother wanted. However, not only would he not trade him for it, he didn't even tell him about it. Then, of all things, a week or so later, he got another one. And again, silence.

Nearly twenty years later, the older brother was in seminary, preparing for the ministry, and needed an illustration of grace. As he thought deeply about it, the generosity, the unselfish-

Grace is a gift—one we cannot buy. ness—the grace—of his younger brother came back to him in full force. That was what his brother had given him. Grace. He didn't earn the baseball card. He couldn't buy it. He got it the only way he could have gotten it. His brother gave it to him.

Ashamed of his own selfishness, he went to his closet, dug out the baseball card collection that hadn't even been thought of in over a decade, found the special cards his younger brother wanted, selected one, wrapped it, and sent it with kind words of thanks.

Grace is a gift, an overflow of generosity. If we try to pay for it, it drains our resources and insults the giver.

Why Is Grace Necessary?

Grace is necessary because we cannot be good enough to earn our salvation.

People are often astonished to hear that how good you are in life has nothing whatsoever to do with whether or not you go to heaven. This has been mentioned before in this book, but it bears repeating. No one has ever been good enough to get into heaven if he did not trust in Jesus, and no one has ever been bad enough to be kept out of heaven if he did trust in Jesus. "Goodness" is not the standard by which a person gets into heaven. Rather, perfection is. If goodness were the standard, we could compare ourselves with others and perhaps squeak into heaven on our own credit. But, since perfection is the standard, we must compare ourselves with God, and when we do that, no one makes it.

Therefore, if we are to get into heaven, we must be made perfect. But how? God's perfection is credited to us when we believe in Jesus and commit our lives to Him. In that act of faith, we are crucified with Christ (Galatians 2:20) so that our old self dies in Him, and we are born again (John 3:7), recreated in Christ in holiness and righteousness (Ephesians 4:24). Why would God do that? Because He loves us. Out of His love, He gives us the gift of grace. No other gift is sufficient to save us.

Let me repeat an illustration I have used elsewhere in this series. Imagine you are a glass manufacturer responsible for the windshield in a space shuttle. The shuttle faces such heat and pressure returning to earth from orbit that the windshield must be perfect to withstand the stress. As you manufacture the windshield under exacting specifications, something unexplainable happens. There is a minute crack in one corner of the glass.

Nothing but perfection can earn our salvation.

You have put so much time and effort into the production of the windshield up to this point that you decide to go ahead and install it. As the government inspectors come around, they spot the crack and disqualify the windshield.

"But," you protest, "it's only a small crack. And it happened early in the manufacturing process. We completed the process, shipped it to the shuttle construction site, and installed it without another thing happening. There are no other cracks, and the one that is there did not get any larger. And, I will never crack another one! Cut me some slack. I've tried so hard!"

What would you do if you were the government inspector? You would tell the manufacturer that you appreciate his effort, but that the windshield must be perfect, and nothing else will do. All other arguments short of perfection are irrelevant and a waste of time. The only thing the manufacturer can do is go back, melt down the special glass, re-cast the mold, and make a new windshield that is perfect.

And so it is with us. We must be perfect, not just good, and if we are not perfect, all other arguments for heaven are irrelevant. We must be made new—made perfect—and that is what Jesus, by His grace, offers to do for each of us (Ephesians 2:1–10).

What Is the Price of Grace?

Grace costs the believer his pride and cost Jesus His life.

It is often said that grace is free, and in a sense it is. We cannot pay for it. But it does cost us something—our pride. If we are

not willing to admit that we are sinners, incapable of saving ourselves, that we need a savior, and to submit ourselves to God, we
cannot receive His grace.

This is both ridiculously difficult and ridiculously easy. It is
difficult in that, if a person is not willing to admit his need, his inability to save himself, then it is impossible to come to Christ.
There are many people who believe in God, believe in heaven and
hell, believe that Jesus is the Son of God, but who don't believe

**Receiving God's
grace can be easy
or impossible.**
that they are so bad that they will go to hell.
They have not committed adultery, or killed
anyone, or sexually molested anyone, or sold
drugs to minors, or any other terrible sin. They
are decent, law-abiding citizens who go to church (or perhaps they
don't), who try to do unto others as they would like others to do
to them, and they simply can't bring themselves to believe that
they will go to hell when they die. They compare themselves with
the rest of humanity, rather than the perfection of God, and conclude (erroneously) that they are in good standing before God.

But, the book of Romans says that all have sinned and come
short of the glory of God (3:23) and that the wages of sin is death
(6:23). If you put those two passages together, we are forced to
admit that everyone dies, spiritually. Everyone is destined for
hell, unless he accepts the only avenue of escape provided by
God: salvation by grace through faith in Jesus. For those unwilling to accept such a statement, to admit such a need, receiving
the grace of God is more than hard—it's impossible.

However, to those who are willing to accept and receive this
truth, receiving God's grace is ridiculously easy. I recall vividly
when I became a Christian as a college student. It was not difficult for me to admit I was a sinner. I knew full well I was. Even I
didn't agree with the lifestyle I was living, but I seemed powerless to change it. If someone had said that in order to be saved, I
had to start digging a hole to China during the day, and at night,
put on a camel-hair robe and, with a candle in my hand, walk up
and down stone-lined hallways in a monastery, chanting mono-
phonic hymns, I would have only had two questions: where's
the shovel, and where's the candle? I knew I needed to be saved
from my sins. I knew I was powerless to save myself. And I was
willing to do whatever necessary to be saved.

In fact, when people told me that I just had to believe in and
receive Jesus as my savior and commit myself to living for Him,

it seemed too easy. I thought there was something I would have to do. In fact, I *wanted* to do something, to demonstrate my sincerity. Just to say "yes," just to accept, just to believe didn't seem adequate. It made me nervous. I wondered if I had been given the whole story.

Yes, the grace of God costs us something. It costs us our pride—our insistence on believing that we don't need to be saved, or that we can save ourselves.

What it costs us, however, pales in comparison to what it cost Jesus. As a member of the Trinity, he was enjoying the pleasures of heaven, the worship of angels, and the glory of His heavenly life. Then, in order to purchase our redemption, He came to earth, took on the form of a man, Jesus of Nazareth, told people of their lost condition and offered to save them. In return, they mocked Him, they ridiculed Him, they rejected Him. Finally, they arrested Him, beat Him, and ultimately killed Him.

> **Grace is free, but it costs us our pride.**

What seemed like His defeat, however, was ultimately His victory, for it was only through His death that He could save us. His death now can count for ours. If we believe in Jesus and receive Him as our personal savior by faith, God will credit Jesus' death for ours, so that we don't have to die, and will credit Jesus' righteousness to us so that we can be vindicated before God. He causes us to be born again so that our old self is done away with and a new self, created in holiness and righteousness, is born.

Yes, in a sense, grace is free, but only free to us. It cost Jesus His life, and it will cost us our pride if we want to receive His grace.

What Is the Result of Grace?

The result of grace is that we are completely accepted by God.

Philip Yancey in *What's So Amazing About Grace?* tells several modern parables to help us grasp the various dimensions of grace. In one parable, a homeless person living on the docks in New York City finds a lottery ticket early one morning as he is scrounging the dumpsters for breakfast. It turns out to be the winning ticket. He will receive hundreds of thousands of dollars a year for the next twenty years. From the edge of starvation, he will never know hunger again. From absolute poverty to almost unspendable wealth overnight: that is a picture of grace.

A Los Angeles entrepreneur's business scheme goes bust, and he loses a million dollars of someone else's money—a sum he could never repay. Certain that he is financially ruined, the entrepreneur goes to his investor with a hopeless repayment scheme. The investor said, "Repayment? Don't be silly. I'm a speculator. I win some, I lose some. I knew your plan had risks. It was a good idea, though, and it's hardly your fault [that the idea didn't work]. Just forget it." Another picture of grace.

A small town girl gets tired of her restrictive lifestyle and takes off for the big city. She is attractive and begins living an opulent lifestyle as a upscale prostitute. After a while, she gets sick, and her "boss" throws her out on the street. Broken physically, emotionally, and spiritually, she lives the death-defying life of a girl on the streets until she finally decides to try to go home. She leaves a message on her parents' answering machine saying that if they want to see her, they should meet her at the bus station at midnight that night. If they don't meet her, she'll get back on the bus and keep going. Tension mounts as the bus pulls into the terminal. She doesn't know if her mom and dad will be there or not. The fifteen-minute stop will determine the rest of her life. None of the possible scenarios she envisions prepares her for what she sees when she walks through the terminal doors. There, against the concrete block walls, stands a group of forty brothers and sisters and aunts and uncles and cousins and a grandmother and great-grandmother. They are all wearing silly party hats and blowing noisemakers, and taped across the entire wall of the terminal is a sign that reads, "Welcome home!" Another picture of grace.

These contemporary stories help us see grace from the standpoint of the one who received grace. Jesus told many parables, including the parable of the prodigal son. But rather than emphasizing the son who received grace, this parable highlights the father who gives grace. The father in this parable represents God, and the parable is really more about the father's love than the son's misbehavior. As Jesus tells the story, the son of a wealthy farmer and businessman demands his inheritance and promptly squanders it in dissipated living. Face down on the sidewalk of life, he decides to return to his father, confess his sin, and ask for forgiveness, hoping to be made one of his father's hired servants. But during the time the wastrel son was gone, his father's eyes have roamed the horizon day after day, hoping

The parable of the prodigal highlights the father's grace.

against hope to catch a glimpse of his lost son coming home—the son for whom he grieved daily—the son whose departure left a permanent hole in his heart. When the longed-for day finally came, the familiar silhouette of the wayward son was still a long way off, walking toward the house. His father ran to him, barely letting him apologize before fitting him with a new suit of clothes, placing a ring on his finger, and throwing a homecoming party. Joy reigned supreme. His lost son was found, and nothing could stay the father's joy.

The parable of the lost son is found in a series of three parables, all of which tell the story of something lost—a lost sheep, a lost coin, and a lost son. The point of each parable is the same. A profound sense of loss, is followed by a dramatic moment of rediscovery, and then by boundless jubilation. These amazing parables tell us what it feels like to be God in that situation. As the sheep is to the shepherd, as the coin is to the woman, and as the son is to the father, so are we to God! We are the center of His attention. We are the focus of His life. We are the dominant matter in His existence. We are lost, and it is almost as though His heart will break unless we are found.

God's grace includes no catch or loophole.

How can this be? How can God care so about us? How can we, who view ourselves as so unlovely, be so loved by the great lover of the universe? Grace! God's grace is the wellspring of overflowing, unstinting, enthusiastic, joyful generosity that includes His passionate desire for our friendship.

As modern Americans, we are used to hype, to sham, to slick talk. We open the sweepstakes envelope that shouts on the outside, "YOU HAVE DEFINITELY WON $1,000,000!!!" only to find the hidden words, "if you should happen to return the winning entry form." "We are accustomed to finding a catch in every promise," Yancey writes. "But Jesus' stories of extravagant grace include no catch, no loophole disqualifying us from God's love. Each has at its core an ending too good to be true—or so good that is must be true" (52).

It would be grace if God were only to spare us the just consequences of our lifelong rebellion against Him. But however gracious mere forgiveness is (and it is wonderful!), forgiveness alone does not fully define or describe the wonders of God's grace. Beyond forgiveness, God reaches out to us in Christ to start an incredible eternal friendship. He welcomes us into a family where He does not merely put up with us, but He positively delights in us as His children.

His love is not a grim "I'm going to forgive you, but you better never forget what I've done and be careful not to get Me upset again." That would be grace with a whiplash—dishonoring to pin on God. But the grace with which God overflows aches for you and me in our empty rebellion against Him. This grace searches us out with no thought of what it will cost the Father to find us (no less than the giving up of His dear Son!).

By grace we are accepted into God's family.

Grace turns heaven into a party when we are found, and grace celebrates our new and unending life together with the One who has only kindness and blessing in mind for us forever (Ephesians 2:4–10). That's amazing, and that's grace!

What Should Our Response Be to God's Grace?

Our response to God's grace should be gratitude, obedience, and joy.

It is a profound understatement to say that a person should be grateful for being saved from eternal destruction and given the promise of heaven and eternal fellowship with God. One escapes the ultimate punishment and receives the ultimate reward. No one in touch with reality could help but be extremely grateful.

Gratitude is dear to the heart of God. I will skew the details to protect the identity in a story that points out the value of gratitude. My nephew was in a fix, and no one could help him except my wife and me. We committed a good bit of time and money to help him in a way that will benefit him for the rest of his life. We were willing to do it simply because he was our nephew. No reward was required. But afterward he came to us and expressed deep and sincere thanks to us for what we had done. We said, "Steve, we were willing to help you even if you hadn't been grateful. But it means a lot to us that you are."

We can't thank God enough—but we should thank Him.

I'm sure the same is true with God. There is much that God does for us that we don't even grasp. We cannot be, we do not have the capability to be, as grateful to God as we ought. His blessings go beyond our comprehension. But if we are anything like God (and in some ways we are), then it means a lot to God for us to express to him our thanks and gratitude.

In addition, we should be obedient to what God asks of us. It is He who has saved us by His grace. But He has not merely saved us *from* something. He has saved us *to* something. He wants our lives to reflect the One who saved us, the God we worship, the God we serve. That requires obedience to His instructions and commands.

Yet, His commands are not a burden (1 John 5:3). Jesus Himself said, "My yoke is easy and my burden light" (Matthew 11:30). In Psalm 1, David wrote that the person who delights and meditates on the word of God would be like a tree planted by rivers of water, bringing forth fruit, not withering, and prospering in whatever he does. In Psalm 19 we read that the word of God is more to be desired than gold, it is sweeter than honey, and that in being obedient to the Scripture, **Our obedience and joy are evidences of God's grace.** there is great reward. Further, in Psalm 119, we read that the one who is obedient to the commands of God is blessed. So, while there is a price to pay for being obedient to the Word of God (we must often go contrary to our inclinations or natural desires), yet there is a higher (negative) price to pay for disobedience.

Finally, we should experience joy. I think God wants most of us to be happier and experience more joy than we do. I think one reason is that we tend to focus on this world rather than the next. As a result, we are often ungrateful for things God has not given us in this world, rather than grateful for what He has given us. If we were to change our focus of gratitude for what He has given us, not only in this world, but also in the next, joy would bubble up and well over in our hearts to a degree that most of us do not experience.

Conclusion

You might as well give in to grace. It is a fact, so you might as well enjoy it. God loves you. He accepts you. You belong to Him. In Christ, you are totally accepted.

I find it almost impossible to be somber at communion. I want to dance and shout and sing. I never do, of course—some think it wouldn't be proper—but I feel like it. I'm so happy to be able to take communion. I'm so happy I belong to the community of people who have the right to take communion freely.

I used to feel vaguely guilty taking communion. I used to think to myself, *What am I doing taking communion? I don't deserve this. I don't belong. I'm not spiritual like these other people.* But no longer. I've taken the plunge. I've chosen to believe the Bible. I've decided to accept God's grace, not just for heaven, but for daily life. And taking communion is one of the privileges that is given to me by the grace of God.

When I first became a Christian, I attended a church where it was fashionable to make communion a time of deep, almost morbid introspection. Great warnings were given before communion not to take it unworthily. Everyone was solemn, as though attending the funeral of a young person who died unexpectedly. We went up front to take communion, and when we knelt at the altar rail, it was common for people to anguish and cry. I used to think that's what spiritual people did, and that if I didn't I wasn't spiritual. I thought I could show Jesus how seriously I took His death for me by working up enough remorse for my sin and enough identification of his pain to bring me to tears at the moment I was to take the bread and the cup.

Grace makes communion a cause for celebration. Now, however, communion is a time of rejoicing for me. Certainly there is a place for introspection and taking the death of Jesus seriously. Certainly it is important to confess unconfessed sin before taking communion. Certainly there may be times when one might dwell on the pain of the crucifixion. But I had fallen into making it a requirement for successful communion. I had to somehow work up the tears each time, and that became more and more difficult.

Over a period of several years, when I finally began to understand and accept some of the grace of God, I lost my ability to work up the tears. Joy took over, and I left that morose mindset behind. Now, I dwell more on the gratitude and joy I have at being one who is qualified to take communion by being in Christ. The overall impact of having accepted the grace of God in my life has been to change communion from a funeral to a celebration in my heart.

If we will but accept who we are in Christ—who God says we are in Scripture—we can have such peace, such security, such confidence, such a sense of belonging in the presence of God, and we can have it forever, beginning now. It may take some time for the idea to grow on us, but if we accept it by faith now, the idea can begin to grow and keep growing.

Speed Bump

Slow down to be sure you've gotten the main points from this chapter.

Question
Answer

Q1. What is grace?

A1. Grace is God's *acceptance* of you and blessing on you, even though you have not earned it.

Q2. Why is grace necessary?

A2. Grace is necessary because we cannot be *good* enough to earn our salvation.

Q3. What is the price of grace?

A3. Grace costs the believer his *pride* and cost Jesus His *life.*

Q4. What is the result of grace?

A4. The result of grace is that we are completely *accepted* by God.

Q5. What should our response be to God's grace?

A5. Our response to God's grace should be gratitude, obedience, and *joy.*

Fill in the Blank

Question
Answer

Q1. What is grace?

A1. Grace is God's _____ of you and blessing on you, even though you have not earned it.

Q2. Why is grace necessary?

A2. Grace is necessary because we cannot be _____ enough to earn our salvation.

Q3. What is the price of grace?

A3. Grace costs the believer his _____ and cost Jesus His _____.

Q4. What is the result of grace?

A4. The result of grace is that we are completely _____ by God.

Q5. What should our response be to God's grace?

A5. Our response to God's grace should be gratitude, obedience, and _____.

For Further Thought and Discussion

1. Have you ever tried to become perfect in thought, motive, word, and deed? If you have, what was the result? If you haven't, what do you think the result would be if you did?

2. If you think the result would be failure, what does this tell you about your need for God's grace?

3. Why do you think more people are not willing to accept God's grace for salvation? Why do you think more people are not willing to rest in God's grace and enjoy their relationship with Him after they are saved?

4. Is it hard for you to accept that God's grace is greater than your sin? Why or why not?

5. Do you think that you are entering into the joy of your relationship with God as fully as you could? If so, what has helped you the most? If not, what is holding you back the most?

What If I Don't Believe?

If I don't believe in the grace of God, I am stunted in my capacity to rest in God, to enjoy belonging to Him, and to take joy in my Christian experience. I may be condemned to trying to earn my acceptance with God, which is like chasing the end of a rainbow—you never arrive. I may fear the loss of my salvation or carry around unresolved guilt. And finally, I am not a magnet to attract others to Christ.

For Further Study

1. Scripture

- Romans 3:23
- Romans 5:1–2
- Romans 6:23
- Romans 11:6
- Galatians 5:19–20
- Ephesians 2:1–10

- Titus 3:5

- Hebrews 12:5–11

2. Books

Joy that Lasts, Gary Smalley
Lifetime Guarantee, Bill Gilliam
Future Grace, John Piper
In the Grip of Grace, Max Lucado
Grace Awakening, Charles Swindoll
What's So Amazing about Grace? Philip Yancey

The glory of God, and, as our only means to glorifying Him, the salvation of human souls, is the real business of life.
■ C.S. Lewis

12

How Can We Share Our Salvation?

I like to share good things I know about. If I discover a good restaurant, I enjoy encouraging people to eat there. I found a mail-order company that has great shirts in sizes to fit anyone from a bull-dog to a gorilla, in a hundred different colors at reasonable prices. I enjoy telling other men about it. There's an automotive repair shop in town run by a Christian. They do excellent work at fair prices, and you can trust them to do the right thing with your car. You don't have to worry about their replacing a loose spark plug wire and charging you $500 for it. They have a clean, pleasant waiting area and they always treat you with respect. I enjoy telling other people about the place. I figure I'm doing them a favor by letting them know about it.

Since I enjoy sharing good news with others, it came naturally for me to want to share my experience of salvation with others when I became a Christian. There is a radio preacher (if you listen to him, you know who I mean) who says (tongue firmly in cheek) that some new Christians ought to be locked up for two years after their conversion and only be let out when they have quit being obnoxious and grabbing people by the lapels and shouting the gospel in their faces. I was one of the ones that needed to be locked up. I shared my faith with nearly every important person in my life, and many others as well. I was a loose cannon on a rocking deck.

But it didn't take long for that to change. Because I shared the gospel indiscriminately with people who weren't ready to hear it, I got a lot of rejection. I heard a non-Christian tell another Christian one time that if the gospel were really true, then every Christian ought to spend every waking hour telling others about it. Because the Christians he knew didn't do that, he thought they were hypocrites and decided that was a reason not to believe the message.

My response is that if he had been rejected as often and as un-kindly as I have been, he would understand why most Christians don't go around grabbing everyone they pass and telling them the gospel. You quickly get a reputation as a nut.

In this chapter we learn that . . .

1. Evangelism is sharing the good news that God loves us and will save us from our sins if we believe in Him and give our lives to Him.
2. The power of our personal story is that when we tell other people of our experience with Christ, they cannot deny it.
3. I can tell my story more effectively by determining how God has gifted me to tell it, rather than feeling locked in to how someone else does it.

On the other hand, too often we overreact and stop telling people altogether. We clam up and become invisible Christians. The answer, of course, lies somewhere in between. While we don't need to go screaming the gospel down the street, we do need to share the gospel with others. So, how do we adopt a lifestyle that includes effective sharing of the message of salvation with others?

What Is Evangelism?

Evangelism is sharing the good news that God loves us and will save us from our sins if we believe in Him and give our lives to Him.

It has been said that the gospel is so simple that a child can understand it, yet so profound that the greatest scholar cannot plumb its depths. What must we do to be saved? Believe in Jesus (Acts 16:31). How can we be born again? Believe in Jesus (John 3:16). How can we become children of God? Believe in and re-ceive Jesus (John 1:12).

Of course, as we have already seen, this believing means more than just knowing or agreeing intellectually with some-thing. It means a commitment of one's life to Jesus. But it is so simple that a young child can become a Christian. I have a friend whose four-year-old son was sitting with his older brother and parents at the breakfast table one morning in a very sullen mood. When asked what was wrong, he said, "Everyone's going to heaven around here but me."

The father said, "Well, then you had better do something about it." A day or two later, the boy said, "I want to accept Jesus into my heart." So they talked about it, and he prayed to receive Christ. That four-year-old is an adult now, involved in Christian ministry, and he remembers that event very clearly as the moment he became a Christian.

Why I Need to Know This

I need to know this so that I can understand what the message of the gospel is, and so that I will accept the mandate to share the gospel with others that is placed on me by the Scriptures.

Yet, the libraries of the world are filled with books trying to explain and understand how God could become man, how His death could count for ours, how the sin of the world could be put on a holy God without destroying the holiness of the godhead, and how it is true that we are elect before the foundation of the world, and yet, whoever will may come. A child can understand enough to be saved, but no one can fully understand the mystery of the gospel of salvation by grace through faith in Jesus.

The message of the gospel of salvation was born in the heart of God before the world was even created. Revelation 13:8 speaks of the "Lamb slain from the foundation of the world," and Ephesians 1:4 teaches that God "chose us in Him before the foundation of the world." The salvation of humanity was in the heart of God even before Adam and Eve rebelled in the garden. God offered salvation to Adam and Eve (Genesis 3:21); He offered it to Cain and Abel (Genesis 4:4–7). He offered it to Abraham (Genesis 12:1–3), and He chose the nation of Israel as His instrument to reach the nations of the world (Psalm 67). The prophet Isaiah tells of the coming Messiah who will come to save His people from their sin (53). Then, Jesus comes on the scene, claiming to be the Messiah. Yes, the gospel has been in the heart of God from the beginning.

Salvation has been in the heart of God from the beginning.

Jesus made it clear that His entire mission in life was to offer salvation to humanity. In Luke 19:10, we read, "For the Son of Man has come to seek and to save that which was lost." His parables focused on salvation. In Luke chapter 15, Jesus taught three parables—about a lost sheep, a lost coin, and a lost son. In each one, the point was that God is not satisfied until that which is lost has been found. God is committed to offering, calling, wooing humanity to accept His offer of salvation.

After Jesus chose the twelve men who were to become His closest disciples, He said, "The harvest is plentiful, but the laborers are few; therefore beseech the Lord of the harvest to send out laborers into His harvest" (Luke 10:2). This set the tone for much of His ministry and teaching. In many of His personal encounters with people, His goal seemed to be to bring them to a point of decision about Him and about their sin. For example, even the rather innocent act of drawing water from a well to get a drink was used by Jesus to evangelize a needy woman (John 4).

When Jesus hung on the cross dying, He cried out, "It is finished" (John 19:30). But what was finished? There were still sick people to heal, blind to give sight to, lame who needed to walk, and hungry folk to feed. So what was finished?

His primary task on earth, namely His death in substitution for the death of all who would believe in Him (John 1:12), is what was finished. Then, after His resurrection, Jesus appeared to His disciples and charged them to go into all the world and proclaim that good news (Matthew 28:19–20).

His disciples took up this mandate with great resolve. Everywhere they went, they preached, often in the face of great resistance and even persecution. When they were beaten and commanded by religious leaders to stop preaching, their response was, "We must obey God rather then men (Acts 5:29). When they were thrown in jail for preaching the gospel, they began preaching again almost the minute they got out (Acts 12:4; 16:23). Thousands came to know Christ through their evangelism (Acts 2:41).

This dedication to spreading the gospel to the ends of the earth has been passed down from one generation to another for the last two thousand years, and still exists today. Certainly many Christians do not have this commitment, but there have always been some committed to world evangelism. Our task in this chapter is to come to the point at which each of us realizes that we should be part of that task force. No one can claim to follow Christ obediently without accepting the responsibility to spread this wonderful message to those who have never heard.

> **Jesus charged His disciples to carry on His mission.**

One of the things that holds us back is that many of us have never fully accepted the grace of God in our everyday lives, and therefore we do not have the joy that motivates us to share the good news with others. One goal of this book is to help us understand God's grace fully enough to realize that we have a story to tell to others, even if we are not perfect.

What Is the Power of Our Personal Story?

The power of our personal story is that when we tell other people of our experience with Christ, they cannot deny it.

Throughout Scripture, it is common for Christ's followers to simply tell others their experience with Jesus. In John 9:25, a blind man whom Jesus had healed was being interrogated about who Jesus was. He said, "All I know is that once I was blind and now I can see." The apostle Paul in Acts 22 was being held by religious leaders who felt he had broken the Law. Paul's defense was simply a recounting of his conversion and subsequent experience with the Lord. The apostle Peter once was detained by the religious leaders, who were demanding that he stop preaching the gospel. His reply? "We cannot but speak the things which we have seen and heard" (Acts 4:20).

Certainly doctrines and creeds have an important role. Often, however, it is not the doctrines and creeds that win people to Christ, but the impact of our lives and our own story of conversion and walk with the Lord.

It used to be that facts and truth could be argued. However, the younger generations today have been reared and educated in an environment that says, "There is no absolute truth." Therefore, they are often not interested in hearing logical arguments for the existence of God or for the truth of Christianity as opposed to other religions or no religion at all. They don't believe you have the right to claim absolute truth. But they will listen to your story, and they cannot refute your experience. So, if the Christian tells his story of conversion and new life in Christ in terms that are rooted both in life experience and in the truth of the Bible, it can be very persuasive.

Even if "truth" is considered irrelevant, your story can't be refuted.

Alister McGrath, in his book *How Shall We Reach Them*, has observed that for many people a concern with the truth is irrelevant. "The first question people tend to ask these days is not, 'Is this right?' but, 'What will this do for me?'" (45). In the last twenty-five years, people who claim to have the truth have come to be viewed as "narrow-minded, petty and authoritarian."

So, how do we deal with this somewhat astonishing and disconcerting development? Well, it does no good to raise our voices and shout that there is, too, absolute truth, and we have it. But there are two things we can do. We can continue to tell them what the Bible says. The word of God is living and powerful, and will not return to God void—that is, without accomplishing what He intends. In addition, we can emphasize the personal attractiveness of Christianity to the one who has rejected the possibility of absolute truth. We must meet him where he is. Besides being true, the Bible also will do some wonderful things for the individual who believes it and acts on its truths. So, we present its benefits, secure in the knowledge that it is true. The genuine convert will come, by the ministry of the Holy Spirit, to believe in its truth.

How Can I Tell My Story More Effectively?

I can tell my story more effectively by determining how God has gifted me to tell it, rather than feeling locked in to how someone else does it.

In the spring of 1975 I did something I am not very proud of. I was teaching at a Christian college, and in my first year as dean of students I learned that I was responsible to oversee "visitation day." On this day we cancelled classes and all students were to take gospel tracts that we provided and go to the mall or go door-to-door and share their faith with others. I swallowed hard. I found cold turkey evangelism intimidating, having tried it a time or two and gotten roundly rejected. I didn't look forward to it, and neither did the students. I received a good bit of complaining about the requirement.

When I asked for more information on how the day was typically organized, I learned (to my profound relief) that the faculty did not accompany the students. I thought that seemed unfair, but I was so relieved, I stomped all over my sense of unfairness and brought it under swift submission. Some of the students complained bitterly that they were not trained to do this, and that the faculty were not going with them. I repeated the party line I had been given from higher up, and quelled the rebellion. Then I sent them out, while I went and hid in my office.

It was an unfair thing to ask of them—to send them out without any training or any experienced leaders or anyone to give them moral support. These kinds of experiences often permanently turn people off to evangelism.

Not everyone is gifted for one approach to evangelism.

What this approach fails to recognize is that different people are gifted to evangelize in different ways, and when we force people to evangelize in ways for which they are not gifted, it often results in no evangelism at all.

Joe Aldrich, in his book *Gentle Persuasion,* says that 10 percent of believers are gifted to share Christ using the methods taught in almost 100 percent of the classes on personal evangelism. I think this is because we have gotten the idea that "cold turkey" evangelism is the only real kind of evangelism, and so the only ones with the desire and knowledge to teach a class are those gifted to use that approach. But it alienates 90 percent of Christians, turning them into cowering, guilt-ridden fugitives, hiding from typical evangelistic activities.

One of the great tasks of the church today is to mobilize the hiding 90 percent by helping them find ways to evangelize that are natural to them. Can you bake a cherry pie? Because if you can, you can evangelize. One way to evangelize is simply to be so nice to people with whom you come in contact that you will eventually have a natural opportunity to share your faith with them—often because they come right out and ask you.

Many people are hungry for the gospel, but they are more afraid to ask anyone about it than you are to share it. If you can just establish a non-threatening relationship with them, the door will often open to share with them on a level that you are both comfortable with.

Each one of us can have pleasure and confidence in evangelizing, if we do what God has gifted and called us to do, rather than what *others* may have called us to do despite the fact that we are not gifted to do it.

Confidence in evangelizing can come from "being natural."

An important first step in becoming a "natural evangelizer" is to accept responsibility for the Great Commission. In Matthew 28:18–20, Jesus said, "All authority has been given to Me in heaven and on earth. Go therefore and make disciples of all the nations, baptizing them in the name of the Father and of the Son and of the Holy Spirit, teaching them to observe all things that I have commanded you; and lo, I am with you always, even to the end of the age."

This has been dubbed the Great Commission. The mandate to take the gospel to all nations is passed down to each successive generation, including us. Each of us must accept responsibility to do what we can to further the Great Commission. Of course, a prominent evangelist may be furthering the Great Commission by having vast crusades and television specials that reach millions of people. The rest of us will reach fewer. But we all must do what we are gifted to do, even if it is only baking a cherry pie. If that is what God has gifted and called us to do, then that is what He wants us to do.

As you accept responsibility for the Great Commission, you say to yourself, *This command of Christ's is not just for others, it is for me, and I must find a way to participate in it.* Then you ask yourself what you think you could do that might, either directly or indirectly, lead to an opportunity to share your faith with someone.

I will never forget the power of a smile on me. When I was in high school, the first contact I can remember having with a family that was biblically Christian in their behavior was at a friend's house. We were playing basketball and got hot and sweaty. My friend suggested we go in and get a drink of water. As we entered the kitchen, I saw his mother for the first time. She was washing dishes, but she turned and smiled at me as I entered. That had **A smile can begin to open a heart.** never happened to me before. I remember thinking, *What a pleasant lady!* Deep down inside, a desire was born in me to have a home like that someday. That smile was not all it took to bring me to Christ a number of years later, but it played a part in my decision.

I believe that each of us needs to be able to share our faith verbally when the opportunity comes, but even a smile can set up the opportunity.

So what can you do? Some time back, I became burdened to be more involved in evangelism, but I was working out of my home at the time, spending most of my life behind a computer. I wanted to evangelize an acquaintance, but in subtle but very clear ways, he let me know that a frontal assault on him would not work.

Then, one day, around Christmas time, I saw a reading of *A Christmas Carol* on public television. I couldn't get over how good it was, and how well it seemed to prepare the listener's heart for the gospel. I thought to myself, *You know, if you just added an inoffensive presentation of the gospel to the end of that, it would be a very effective tool for evangelism.* So, two friends and I rented a beautiful room in a historic building in town that seated a little over a hundred people. We advertised and packed out two performances. My friend came and enjoyed it. I had the opportunity to share my faith with him in a non-threatening environment. I don't think it could have been done any other way. As far as I know, he has not come to Christ, but that is not my task. I cannot bring others to Christ. I can only tell others about Him.

In contrast, however, I asked a friend of mine who is shy about getting up in front of people whether he would rather jump out of an airplane, play with snakes, or get up in front of a bunch of people and speak. Without hesitation, he said, "First, I'd rather jump out of an airplane; second, I'd rather play with snakes; third, I'd rather get up in front of a bunch of people and speak." Yet this man is very effective sharing his faith one-on-one in the workplace. That just points out the contrast of gifts and calling. He is comfortable doing some things I am not, and I am comfortable doing some things he is not. So we each commit ourselves to the Great Commission, and then we say, "Lord, what can I do? What do You want me to do to advance the Great Commission?" Then, we do what we can.

Each of us must do what we can.

Conclusion

Again, in *Gentle Persuasion*, Joe Aldrich tells a story with which many of us can identify:

> Truck drivers are a breed apart. I learned that the hard way. While laboring over a seminary Hebrew assignment, I became convicted that an "eighteen-wheeler" who lived down a few doors from me needed to be evangelized . . . right now, whether he felt like it or not. I set aside my Hebrew text and waltzed down the sidewalk to his apartment. I could hear the TV blaring as I knocked on his door. It swung open just as the bedroom door closed—his live-in girl friend was there.
>
> I didn't beat around the bush. I asked him to shut off the TV and proceeded to evangelize him. I dumped the whole spiel. Buried the poor soul.

> Contrary to my naive expectations, he wasn't interested in the Bible, Christianity or Christ. He told me so point-blank.
>
> Is it possible that the Lord will use my feeble attempt at evangelizing the trucker? Perhaps. While my approach was probably not the ideal, God's Word does not return void. So should I continue to proceed with such hasty methods? Probably not.
>
> I overlooked some options. He and I lived in the same apartment building. We could have become friends. I could have taken an interest in his world and been more sensitive to his state of readiness. Ruthe and I could have had him over for dinner. Bachelors love home-cooked meals. We could have networked him with other believers in the apartment complex.
>
> As I reflect over that experience, I realize that I missed the opportunity to spend a day traveling with him in the truck. I'd have loved it (169–170).

I have seen gifted evangelists lead people to Christ with just such a brusque approach. In fact, the greatest "soul-winner" I have ever known personally broke all the rules for sharing the gospel with others. But was he ever used by God, in spite of it!

However, most of us are not gifted or comfortable with such a head-on approach. In which case, Aldrich gives another possible approach:

> I recently met a fascinating, radiant Christian from India. His ministry to international students is leading scores of Hindus and Moslems to Christ. What accounts for his effectiveness in reaching members of these radically different cultural and religious traditions?
>
> Each Sunday, he told me, he and his wife host somewhere between thirty and fifty students for dinner. That's a key part of his strategy. Food and camaraderie break down barriers. There's something about eating a meal with someone that accelerates friendship.
>
> "So you talk about Christ at these meals?" I asked.
>
> "No," he said. "It is impossible to talk openly of Jesus Christ."
>
> "So how," I asked him, "are you able to see so many find Christ?"
>
> "I love them," he replied, "until they ask me why" (8).

Ah. There we have an approach that all of us can do. Not necessarily having fifty international people over for dinner every Sunday, but rather, loving the people in our world until they ask us why.

Speed Bump

Slow down to be sure you've gotten the main points from this chapter.

Question
Answer

Q1. What is evangelism?

A1. Evangelism is sharing the *good news* that God loves us and will save us from our sins if we believe in Him and give our lives to Him.

Q2. What is the power of our personal story?

A2. The power of our personal story is that when we tell other people of our *experience* with Christ, they cannot deny it.

Q3. How can I tell my story more effectively?

A3. I can tell my story more effectively by determining how God has *gifted* me to tell it, rather than feeling locked in to how someone else does it.

Fill in the Blank

Question
Answer

Q1. What is evangelism?

A1. Evangelism is sharing the _____ _____ that God loves us and will save us from our sins if we believe in Him and give our lives to Him.

Q2. What is the power of our personal story?

A2. The power of our personal story is that when we tell other people of our _____ with Christ, they cannot deny it.

Q3. How can I tell my story more effectively?

A3. I can tell my story more effectively by determining how God has _____ me to tell it, rather than feeling locked in to how someone else does it.

For Further Thought and Discussion

1. If someone asked you to tell them the gospel in one minute, could you do it? If not, what would you have to do in order to be able to? Is this a goal that you would like to meet? What is the first step you could take to meet it?

2. Have you ever told anyone your story of how you became a Christian? What are the main points of the story?

3. Have you ever accepted personal responsibility for the Great Commission? How do you think you could best contribute to world evangelism?

What if I Don't Believe?

1. If I don't believe that evangelism is important, I turn my back on one of the clearest and most important commands of the Bible. In addition, if I do not feel compassion for the lost, if I do not have the ability to imagine how terrible his life would be if I had never heard the gospel, it would both reflect and encourage an insensitive and hardened heart.

2. If I don't believe my personal story of salvation is important, I lose the opportunity to craft and hone my story (which in itself is a privilege), and lose the opportunities to witness that would come my way if I did.

3. If I don't believe that the most effective way for me to evangelize is to do it the way God has created and gifted me to do it, then I will probably fall into one of two traps. On the one hand, I may become so frustrated with trying to do it the way other people think it should be done that I don't evangelize at all. Or, on the other hand, I may try to do it someone else's way, and be deeply frustrated and possibly ineffective.

For Further Study

1. Scripture

- John 1:12
- John 3:16
- Matthew 28:18–20
- Acts 4:20
- Acts 16:31

2. Books

Gentle Persuasion, Joseph C. Aldrich
The Power of Story, Leighton Ford
How Shall We Reach Them? Michael Green and Alister McGrath

Bibliography

Aldrich, Joseph. *Gentle Persuasion*. Portland, OR: Multnomah Press, 1989.

Barclay, William. *The Letters to Galatians and Ephesians*. Philadelphia: The Westminster Press, 1958.

Erickson, Millard. *Salvation: God's Amazing Plan*. Wheaton, IL: Victor Books, 1978.

Lewis, C.S. *Mere Christianity*. New York: MacMillan, 1952.

McGrath, Alister. *How Shall We Reach Them?* Nashville: Thomas Nelson Publishers, 1995.

Packer, James I. *Concise Theology*. Wheaton, IL: Tyndale, 1993.

Packer, James I. *God Has Spoken*. Downers Grove, IL: InterVarsity Press, 1979.

Piper, John. *Desiring God*. Portland, OR: Multnomah Press, 1986.

Plantinga, Cornelius, Jr. *Not the Way It's Supposed to Be*. Grand Rapids: Eerdman's, 1995.

Schaeffer, Francis. *How Should We Then Live?* Old Tappan, NJ: Fleming H. Revell, 1972.

Stott, John R.W. *The Cross of Christ*. Downers Grove, IL: InterVarsity Press, 1986.

Swindoll, Charles R. *The Grace Awakening*. Dallas: Word, Pub., 1990.

Yancey, Philip. *What's So Amazing About Grace?* Grand Rapids: Zondervan, 1997.

Master Review

Chapter 1

Q1. How does history show that we are lost?

A1. The history of humanity's savagery against itself shows that humanity is lost.

Q2. How does our conscience show that we are lost?

A2. Our conscience shows that we are lost since we are unable to live up to our own standards, let alone God's.

Q3. How does our experience show that we are lost?

A3. The inability of humanity to experience the fullness of its aspirations indicates its lostness.

Q4. How does the death of Christ show that we are lost?

A4. Christ would not have endured the cross if humanity were not lost and in need of salvation.

Q5. What does the Bible say about humanity's lostness?

A5. The Bible says that all have sinned and come short of the glory of God and that the wages of that sin is eternal separation from God.

Chapter 2

Q1. Why did God create in the first place?

A1. God created to reveal His glory.

Q2. Why did God create humanity as He did?

A2. God intended to populate the world with people with whom He could share His love and reveal His glory forever.

Q3. Why did God create the world as He did?

A3. God intended the world to reflect His character and His glory.

Chapter 3

Q1. What is sin?

A1. Sin is anything that does not conform to or that transgresses the will of God.

Q2. Why did Adam and Eve sin?

A2. Adam and Eve sinned because they believed Satan's lie that there was something better to life than what God was giving them.

Q3. What was the effect of sin?

A3. The effect of sin is our alienation from God, from others, from ourselves, and from the created world.

Chapter 4

Q1. How did God respond to the fall of humanity?

A1. God responded to the Fall by saving those who truly believed Him.

Q2. Why did God choose Israel?

A2. God chose Israel as His special people through whom to bring salvation to all the other nations of the world.

Q3. Why did Jesus come?

A3. Jesus came in fulfillment of God's promises to Israel, including the broadening of His covenant to include Gentiles.

Chapter 5

Q1. What is repentance?

A1. Repentance means "changing one's moral direction," turning away from evil.

Q2. What is faith?

A2. Faith is believing what God has said and responding accordingly.

Q3. What is the new birth?

A3. New birth is the transformation from spiritual death to spiritual life.

Chapter 6

Q1. What is justification?

A1. Justification is being declared righteous by God.

Q2. What is adoption?

A2. Adoption is being taken into and made a legal member of another family, as though one were born into that family.

Q3. What is union with Christ?

A3. Union with Christ is to become one with Him spiritually.

Chapter 7

Q1. What is assurance?

A1. Assurance is the confidence that Christians are, in fact, saved.

Q2. What is eternal security?

A2. Eternal security is the belief that genuine Christians will always be saved.

Chapter 8

Q1. How do I join the body?

A1. I join the body by becoming a Christian.

Q2. What is my gift to the body?

A2. My gift to the body is to use my spiritual gift in its behalf.

Q3. What is my Christian duty to the body?

A3. My duty is to commit myself to the body's welfare.

Chapter 9

Q1. What is a Christian's responsibility as a good Samaritan?

A1. A Christian should help those in need who come across his path, and whose need he is able to meet.

Q2. What is a Christian's responsibility as a good citizen?

A2. A Christian should be a good citizen to help establish justice and righteousness in the nation.

Q3. What is a Christian's responsibility as a good neighbor?

A3. A Christian should love his neighbor as himself.

Q4. What is a Christian's responsibility as a good worker?

A4. A Christian should do his job as though he were working for Jesus.

Q5. What is a Christian's responsibility as a beacon of light?

A5. A Christian should be a beacon of light to help make the world a better place in which to live.

Chapter 10

Q1. What does shalom mean?

A1. Shalom means not just an absence of conflict, but the presence of all things as they should be.

Q2. How is shalom thwarted today?

A2. Today, shalom is thwarted by sin.

Q3. How can we help restore shalom?

A3. We can encourage shalom by trying to live life as Jesus would if He were in our shoes.

Chapter 11

Q1. What is grace?

A1. Grace is God's acceptance of you and blessing on you, even though you have not earned it.

Q2. Why is grace necessary?

A2. Grace is necessary because we cannot be good enough to earn our salvation.

Q3. What is the price of grace?

A3. Grace costs the believer his pride and cost Jesus His life.

Q4. What is the result of grace?

A4. The result of grace is that we are completely accepted by God.

Q5. What should our response be to God's grace?

A5. Our response to God's grace should be gratitude, obedience, and joy.

Chapter 12

Q1. What is evangelism?

A1. Evangelism is sharing the good news that God loves us and will save us from our sins if we believe in Him and give our lives to Him.

Q2. What is the power of our personal story?

A2. The power of our personal story is that when we tell other people of our experience with Christ, they cannot deny it.

Q3. How can I tell my story more effectively?

A3. I can tell my story more effectively by determining how God has gifted me to tell it, rather than feeling locked in to how someone else does it.

About the Author

Dr. Max Anders is a pastor at heart who applies the truths of God's word to people's everyday lives. An original team member with Walk Thru the Bible Ministries and pastor of a mega-church for a number of years before beginning his speaking and writing ministry, Max has traveled extensively, speaking to thousands across the country.

His books include *30 Days to Understanding the Bible, 30 Days to Understanding How to Live a Christian Life, 30 Days to Understanding What Christians Believe,* as well as the other titles in this series. He holds a master of theology degree from Dallas Theological Seminary and a doctorate from Western Seminary in Portland, Oregon.

* * *

If you are interested in having Max Anders speak at your conference, church, or special event, please call interAct Speaker's Bureau at 1-800-370-9932.